DRAW ME

Draw Me

*Catholic Prayers for Every Occasion
in a Woman's Life*

Selected by Carmen Rojas

CHARIS

Servant Publications
Ann Arbor, Michigan

Copyright © 1990 by Servant Publications for Introduction and arrangement of prayers.
All rights reserved.

Published by Servant Publications
P.O. Box 8617
Ann Arbor, Michigan 48107

Redeemer Books is an imprint of Servant Publications especially designed to serve Roman Catholics.

Cover Design by Michael Andaloro
Cover Photo by Luci Shaw

    95 96 97 98 10 9 8 7 6 5

Printed in the United States of America
ISBN 0-89283-660-1

Library of Congress Cataloging-in-Publication Data

Draw me : Catholic prayers for every occasion in a woman's life / selected by Carmen Rojas.
      p.   cm.
   "A Redeemer book."
   Includes bibliographical references.
   ISBN 0-89283-660-1
   1. Women—Prayer-books and devotions—English.   2. Catholic Church—Prayer-books and devotions—English.   I. Rojas, Carmen.
BX2170.W7D73 1990
242'.843—dc20   90-30940
                                                                      CIP

Draw Me

Draw me—I will run, run after You.
I will extol Your love—rightly are You loved!
With great delight I sit in Your shadow,
And Your fruit is sweet.
You have brought me to the banquet,
And Love is Your banner
Over me.

I hear Your voice, "Arise, arise, oh My love.
Arise, oh My love, come away, come away with Me.
Winter is passed and the rains are over.
The time of singing has come."
My beloved is mine, And I am His.
I will arise!

Set me as a seal upon Your heart,
As a seal upon Your arm, for love is strong as death.
I am Yours, yes, Yours forever,
And Your desire is for me.
I will give You my love.
I will give You my love,
Oh my King.

Adapted from the Song of Solomon

Contents

Introduction

YOU MUST BECOME LIKE CHILDREN

A child does not find it difficult or complicated to talk to her father, nor does she feel embarrassed to bring her simplest needs to his attention. Children can teach us a great deal about trust. This is why God calls us to be like children in our relationship with him. He reminds us of his fatherly care through Jesus' words: "Or what man of you, if his son asks him for bread, will give him a stone? Or if he asks for a fish, will give him a serpent? If you then, who are evil, know how to give good gifts to your children, how much more will your Father who is in heaven give good things to those who ask him!" (Matthew 7:9-11).

Prayer is one of the primary means by which we allow God to father us. Through prayer, we build the most important relationship of our lives—the love bond between our Maker and ourselves. This link of intimate fellowship gives us access to God's endless supply of riches and wisdom; it centers us in the unshakable identity of being his precious child; it affords us the confidence to risk, to change, to grow, and to love as we live our lives in the shadow of his care. "And this is the confidence which we have in him, that if we ask anything according to his will he hears us. And if we know that he hears us in whatever we ask, we know that we have obtained the requests made of him'' (1 John 5:14, 15).

THE DAUGHTERS OF GOD

When our Maker fashioned women, he created us with a special capacity to love others. A woman can house a baby in her womb and nurture her children with great care. Scripture says that a good wife is worth far more than jewels and her husband trusts in her and gains much from her. A woman has the capacity to form deep and lasting relationships with her friends, to share intimately from her heart, to be loyal even in times of great difficulty. Beyond those in her immediate care, God has given her his heart of compassion for the needy. She can be easily moved to pity and is able to serve the wounded with loving kindness.

The Lord loves his daughters, for he made women to reflect much of his own character and equipped them with the gifts of his love. To God it is not so important that his daughters excel in every talent, but that they give back to him what he first gave to them—love. Just as Jesus delighted that Mary sat at his feet rather than joining Martha as she rushed about, so he delights when we sit in his presence and share our hearts with him.

THE POWER OF A WOMAN'S PRAYERS

That is why the Holy Scriptures speak much about the importance of prayer. Prayer, intimate communion with our loving God, changes us. It changes us from an anxious, hurried, fearful Martha to a contented Mary. It shapes us into our best selves that reflect God's image. Not only does it transform us, it transforms events and circumstances. God wants so much for his daughters to draw near to him that he allows us to change things through prayer. He grants us a partnership with him in directing the course of human history. It is extraordinary to realize that our prayers can change the circumstances of the world around us.

It should not surprise us, then, that prayer is the most important business we have in life. This lifeline to our God is always available to us. It is not hard to grasp or difficult to use. When we draw near to God in prayer, he draws near to us. It is that simple.

WHAT KEEPS US FROM PRAYING?

The life of a woman is often complicated and difficult. Whether we toil in the pressured work world, rear children at home, live with a difficult person, face poverty or illness, we can find our lot burdensome. Loneliness, despair, depression, anxiety, and anger creep into our lives. And under the weight of our responsibilities and burdens we sometimes find that God's voice is difficult to hear. We easily lose sight of his care. Our lifeline appears out of reach in an ocean of difficulties.

Even when our circumstances are not particularly hard, we are often too hurried to find time to contemplate our deep need for God. Only when our self-sufficiency fails us do we realize that we have neglected the One who sustains us. For only he knows our beginning and our end and all that lies between. He wants us to take hold of his hand in prayer so he can transform our lives every day with his goodness.

CREATING A LIFE OF PRAYER

Especially designed for the needs of women of all ages and in all stages of life, this book offers a rich array of prayers that will help you find daily intimacy with God. Here you will discover how to pray about practically every area of your life and more. This book includes prayers on topics such as motherhood, single life, hospitality, service, the poor and needy, busyness, grieving, home life, the work world, friendships, love, and many more. You will learn from extraordinary saints and ordinary people what it means to trust God in all circumstances. If you find it difficult to speak to God, this prayer book shows you how, and more than this, it will give you faith and hope that he will respond to you whenever you approach him.

HOW TO USE THIS CATHOLIC PRAYER BOOK FOR WOMEN

If you use this book as part of your regular prayer life, you will experience God's loving presence and power. Within it you will find prayers from a wide variety of sources, from the saints, from Scripture, from ordinary men and women—all of which can lead you deeper into prayer. Learn from Basilea Schlink, St. Augustine, St. Francis de Sales, Mother Teresa, John of the Cross, St. Francis, Rita Snowden, Pope John Paul II, St. Teresa of Lisieux, Mother Angelica, and many others.

Before you begin to use this book, you will need a sense of how it is organized. The prayers are organized by category under four main sections. For instance, Part I, *Lord, Reign in My Life*, has prayers on hope, forgiveness, strength, and love; while Part II, *Lord, Walk with Me Today*, contains prayers to use in busy times, prayers for your children, work, and health. Part III, *Lord, Comfort Me*, contains prayers for times of depression, grief, trouble, and insecurity. And Part IV, *Lord, Lead Me to Everlasting Life*, is made up of popular Catholic prayers such as the peace prayer by St.

Francis, prayers to the Blessed Mother, prayers before and after confession and communion, morning and evening prayers, and prayers for the dying. It also contains popular Catholic devotionals such as the Rosary and the Stations of the Cross as well as several litanies. These examples are but a sampling of the prayer topics found in the *Draw Me*.

This book is ideal for personal use. You can either use it as a handy reference work to turn to in a moment of need, or you can read through all the prayers under a certain topic for daily prayer and meditation. For example, suppose a young woman is struggling with feelings of inadequacy. She can make a practice of turning to the section in Part III that contains prayers on this topic. Or suppose a mother is concerned about her children and wants to bring their need to God. She can find help by turning to the section on praying for your children in Part II.

During your prayer time, try meditating on these prayers and then freely speak out to God those that are most personally meaningful. Use the prayers as "starters" that help you begin to speak to God, then add to them whatever comes to your mind. Fill in particular details of your life between the lines. For example, "Father, I thank you for my children [for John, Mary, and Phillip]. Grant me grace to love each one of them [especially John when his adolescent behavior grates on my nerves]. Grant me the faithfulness to take care of all their needs [even when I'm feeling tired and not eager to change another diaper]. Give me the wisdom to lead them to your plans for their lives [not mine]. Grant me a deep joy for being their mother. Amen.''

If you want to know how to pray about a specific area of need, this book can show you how. When you find it hard to pray because you are distracted or burdened, it can center your mind and help you persevere. You will find it encouraging to see that many others, whose prayers are collected in this work, have faced much of what you do during the course of life. Learn from them how to love God, grow in faith, find healing, and best of all, hold on to God's lifeline of love and power every day.

However you decide to incorporate *Draw Me* in your life, it will be an invaluable tool as you seek God. After you pray, take time to listen for God's voice in your heart. Don't forget to thank him when he answers your prayers, for he surely will.

—Carmen Rojas

Part I

Lord, Reign in My Life

ONE

Faith

The LORD is my chosen portion and my cup;
  thou holdest my lot.
The lines have fallen for me in pleasant places;
  yea, I have a goodly heritage.

I bless the LORD who gives me counsel;
  in the night also my heart instructs me.
I keep the LORD always before me;
  because he is at my right hand, I shall not be moved.
Therefore my heart is glad, and my soul rejoices;
  my body also dwells secure.
For thou dost not give me up to Sheol,
  or let thy godly one see the Pit.
Thou dost show me the path of life,
  in thy presence there is fulness of joy,
  in thy right hand are pleasures for evermore.

Psalm 16:5-11

Though the fig tree do not blossom,
  nor fruit be on the vines,

the produce of the olive fail
   and the fields yield no food,
the flock be cut off from the fold
   and there be no herd in the stalls,
yet I will rejoice in the LORD,
   I will joy in the God of my salvation.
GOD, my Lord, is my strength;
   he makes my feet like hinds' feet,
   he makes me tread upon my high places.

Habbakuk 3:17-19

Strength and dignity are her clothing,
   and she laughs at the time to come.
She opens her mouth with wisdom,
   the teaching of kindness is on her tongue . . .
"Many women have done excellently,
   but you surpass them all."
Charm is deceitful, and beauty is vain,
   but a woman who fears the LORD is to be praised.
Give her of the fruit of her hands,
   and let her works praise her in the gates.

Proverbs 31:25-26, 29-31

Father,
I abandon myself into your hands;
do with me what you will.
Whatever you may do, I thank you:
I am ready for all, I accept all.
Let only your will be done in me,

and in all your creatures—
I wish no more than this, O Lord.

Into your hands I commend my soul;
I offer it to you with all the love of my heart,
for I love you Lord,
and so need to give myself,
to surrender myself into your hands,
without reserve,
and with boundless confidence,

For you are my Father.   *Charles de Foucauld*

In hope, against all human hope,
    Self desperate, I believe;
Thy quickening word shall raise me up,
    Thou wilt thy Spirit give.

The thing surpasses all my thought,
    But faithful is my Lord;
Through unbelief I stagger not,
    For God hath spoke the word.

Faith, mighty faith, the promise sees,
    And looks at that alone;
Laughs at impossibilities,
    And cries—"It shall be done!"   *Hannah Whitall Smith*

Yours, you made me,
Yours, you saved me,
Yours, you endured me,

Yours, you called me,
Yours, you awaited me,
Yours, I did not stray.
What do You want of me?

Give me then wisdom.
Or for love, ignorance,
Years of abundance,
Or hunger and famine.
Darkness or sunlight,
Move me here or there:
What do You want of me?   *St. Teresa of Avila*

One thing Jesus asks of me: that I lean on Him; that in Him and only in Him I put complete trust; that I surrender myself to Him unreservedly. Even when all goes wrong and I feel as if I am a ship without a compass, I must give myself completely to Him. I must not attempt to control God's action; I must not count the stages in the journey He would have me make. I must not desire a clear perception of my advance upon the road, must not know precisely where I am upon the way of holiness. I ask Him to make a saint of me, yet I must leave to Him the choice of the saintliness itself and still more the means which lead to it.

Mother Teresa of Calcutta

Just for today,
What does it matter, O Lord, if the future is dark?

To pray now for tomorrow—I am not able.
Keep my heart only for today,
   give me your protection today,
   grant me your light—
   just for today.   *St. Thérèse of Lisieux*

What is Faith? It is to understand that this world is not enough for our happiness, to look beyond it on towards God, to realize His presence, to wait upon Him, to endeavor to learn and to do His will, and to seek our good from Him.

To have faith in God is to surrender one's self to God, humbly to put one's interests, or to wish to be allowed to put them, into His hands who is the sovereign Giver of all good.   *John Henry Cardinal Newman*

FAITH is not merely praying
   Upon our knees at night:
Faith is not merely straying
   Through darkness into light:
Faith is not merely waiting
   For glory that may be—
Faith is the brave endeavor,
   The splendid enterprise,
The strength to serve, whatever
   Conditions may arise.   *Anonymous*

TWO

Hope

"For thy power depends not upon numbers, nor thy might upon men of strength; for thou art God of the lowly, helper of the oppressed, upholder of the weak, protector of the forlorn, the savior of those without hope.

"Hear, O hear me, God of my father, God of the inheritance of Israel, Lord of heaven and earth, Creator of the waters, King of all thy creation, hear my prayer!

"And cause thy whole nation and every tribe to know and understand that thou art God, the God of all power and might, and that there is no other who protects the people of Israel but thou alone."

Judith 9:11-12/14

Behold, the eye of the LORD is on those who fear him,
 on those who hope in his steadfast love,
that he may deliver their soul from death
 and keep them alive in famine.
Our soul waits for the LORD;
 he is our help and shield.

Yea, our heart is glad in him,
　　because we trust in his holy name.
Let thy steadfast love, O LORD, be upon us,
　　even as we hope in thee.　*Psalm 33:18-22*

O HEART of love, I put all my trust in You; for I fear all
things from my own weakness, but I hope for all things
from Your goodness.　*Margaret Mary Alacoque*

My Lord God, I have no idea where I am going.
I do not see the road ahead of me.
I cannot know for certain where it will end.
Nor do I really know myself,
and the fact that I think that I am following
　　your will does not mean that I am
　　actually doing so.
But I believe that the desire to please you
　　does in fact please you.
And I hope I have that desire
　　in all that I am doing.
I hope that I will never do anything apart
　　from that desire.
And I know that if I do this,
you will lead me by the right road though I
　　may know nothing about it.
Therefore will I trust you always though I
　　may seem lost and in the shadow
　　of death.
I will not fear, for you are ever with me,

and you will never leave me to face my
    perils alone.   *Thomas Merton*

The Lord will help her; his loving presence will be with
    her.
    —The Lord will help her; his loving presence will be
    with her.
He dwells in her; she will not falter.
    —His loving presence will be with her.
                    Responsory Liturgy of the Hours

My God, you are my anchor
on a stormy sea,
my serenity on a windy night,
my hope when all else fails.
Your presence surrounds me like a
protective shield and when the
arrows of my selfishness pierce through,
Your loving arms extend themselves
to reach out and grasp my wandering soul.
                    Mother Angelica

Lord our God,
under the shadow of Thy wings let us hope.
Thou will support us, both when little and
even to gray hairs.
When our strength is of Thee, it is strength;
but when our own, it is feebleness.
We return to Thee, O Lord,

that from their weariness our souls may rise
towards Thee, leaning on the things which thou
have created, and passing on to Thyself, who
has wonderfully made them;
for with Thee are refreshment and true strength.
Amen.   *St. Augustine of Hippo*

THREE

Love

I love thee, O LORD, my strength.
   The LORD is my rock, and my fortress, and my
      deliverer.
my God, my rock in whom I take refuge,
   my shield, and the horn of my salvation, my
      stronghold.   *Psalm 18:1-2*

Nevertheless I am continually with thee;
   thou dost hold my right hand.
Thou dost guide me with thy counsel,
   and afterward thou wilt receive me to glory.
Whom have I in heaven but thee?
   And there is nothing upon earth that I desire besides
      thee.
My flesh and my heart may fail
   but God is the strength of my heart and my portion
      for ever.   *Psalm 73:23-26*

O God, thou art my God, I seek thee,
   my soul thirsts for thee;

my flesh faints for thee,
as in a dry and weary land where no water is.
So I have looked upon thee in the sanctuary,
beholding thy power and glory.
Because thy steadfast love is better than life,
my lips will praise thee. *Psalm 63:1-3*

". . . You shall love the LORD your God with all your heart, and with all your soul, and with all your might. And these words which I command you this day shall be upon your heart; and you shall teach them diligently to your children, and shall talk of them when you sit in your house, and when you walk by the way, and when you lie down and when you rise. And you shall bind them as a sign upon your hand, and they shall be as frontlets between your eyes. And you shall write them on the doorposts of your house and on your gates."
Deuteronomy 6:5-9

Make us hunger and thirst for You with our whole hearts. With all our longings let us desire You. Make us serve You—You, alone—with all of our heart. With all our zeal help us desire only those things that are pleasing to You. *St. Anselm of Canterbury*

My God, because You are so good, I love You with all my heart, and for Your sake I love my neighbor as myself.
If I love You, Lord, it is not just because of heaven

which You have promised; if I fear to offend You, it is not because hell threatens me.

What draws me to you, O Lord, is Yourself alone, it is the sight of You, nailed to the cross for me, Your body bruised in the pains of death.

Your love so holds my heart that, if there were no heaven, I would love You still. If there were no hell I would even still fear to offend You.

I do not need Your gifts to make me love You, for even if I should have no help of hope at all of all the things I do hope for, I would still love You with that very same love. Amen.   *St. Teresa of Avila*

O GOD! You are life, wisdom, truth, goodness and happiness. You are the eternal, the only true good. My Lord and my God! You are my hope and the joy of my heart. I profess it and thank You that You have fashioned me in Your own image, so that I may fix all my thoughts on You and ever love You.

Grant, O Lord, that I may truly realize that I may ever love You more and more and joyfully possess You. And, as I cannot fully win this happiness in the life here below, grant at least that it may grow in me day by day, until it is fully realized in the life to come.

St. Anselm of Canterbury

Late have I loved you,
O Beauty so ancient and so new;
late have I loved you!

For behold you were within me,
and I outside;
and I sought you outside
and in my unloveliness
fell upon those lovely things
that you have made.
You were with me
and I was not with you.
I was kept from you by those things,
yet had they not been in you
they would not have been at all.
You did call and cry to me
and break open my deafness;
and you sent forth your beams
to shine upon me
and chase away my blindness.
You breathed fragrance upon me,
and I drew in my breath
and do now pant for you;
I tasted you
and now hunger and thirst for you.
You touched me,
and I burned for your peace.   *St. Augustine of Hippo*

You wish me to tell you why God should be loved, and
in what way or measure we should love Him?

I answer then:

The reason for our loving God is God, and the measure of loving God is to love Him without measure.

St. Bernard of Clairvaux

The soul of one who loves God always swims in joy, always keeps holiday, and is always in a mood for singing.   *St. John of the Cross*

FOUR

Forgiveness

And as they were stoning Stephen, he prayed, "Lord Jesus, receive my spirit." And he knelt down and cried with a loud voice, "Lord, do not hold this sin against them." And when he had said this, he fell asleep.

Acts 7:59-60

Then Peter came up and said to him, "Lord, how often shall my brother sin against me, and I forgive him? As many as seven times?" Jesus said to him, "I do not say to you seven times, but seventy-times seven."

Matthew 18:21-22

He that takes vengeance will suffer vengeance from
    the Lord,
  and he will firmly establish his sins.
Forgive your neighbor the wrong he has done,
  and then your sins will be pardoned when you pray.
Does a man harbor anger against another,
  and yet seek for healing from the Lord?

Does he have no mercy toward a man like himself,
   and yet pray for his own sins?
If he who himself, being flesh, maintains wrath,
   who will make expiation for his sins?
Remember the end of your life, and cease from enmity,
   remember destruction and death, and be true to the
      commandments.
Remember the commandments, and do not be angry
      with your neighbor;
   remember the covenant of the Most High, and
overlook ignorance.   *Sirach 28:1-7*

Put on then, as God's chosen ones, holy and beloved,
compassion, kindness, lowliness, meekness, and patience, forbearing one another and, if one has a com-
plaint against another, forgiving each other; as the Lord
has forgiven you, so you also must forgive. And above
all these put on love, which binds everything together
in perfect harmony.   *Colossians 3:12-14*

O Almighty God, give to your servant a meek and
gentle spirit, that I may be slow to anger, and easy to
mercy and forgiveness. Give me a wise and constant
heart, that I may never be moved to an intemperate
anger for any injury that is done or offered. Lord, let me
ever be courteous, and easy to be entreated; let me
never fall into a peevish or contentious spirit, but
follow peace with all men; offering forgiveness, inviting
them by courtesies, ready to confess my own errors, apt

to make amends, and desirous to be reconciled. Let no sickness or cross accident, no employment or weariness, make me angry or ungentle and discontented, or unthankful, or uneasy to them that minister to me; but in all things make me like unto the holy Jesus—Amen.
Bishop Jeremy Taylor

O God of love, who has given a new commandment, through Your Only-begotten Son, that we should love one another, even as You have loved us, the unworthy and the wandering, and gave Your beloved Son for our life and salvation; we pray to You, Lord, give to us Your servants, in all time of our life on the earth, a mind forgetful of past ill-will, a pure conscience and sincere thoughts, and a heart to love our brothers and sisters— Amen.   *Coptic Liturgy of St. Cyril*

O Eternal Father, help me, I beseech You, to bring forth in my life the fruits of the Spirit; the fruit of Love, that I may love You above all things, and all others in You and for Your sake; the fruit of Joy, that I may find Your service my delight; the fruit of Peace, that, pardoned and accepted through Your mercy, I may repose in Your love; the fruit of Long-suffering, that I may bear, with patient submission to Your will, all crosses and afflictions; the fruit of Gentleness, that I may subdue all risings of temper, and take calmly and sweetly all trials and provocations; the fruit of Meekness, that I may forgive freely all who may hurt me either by word or deed, and endure with patience all that may be laid upon me; the fruit of Temperance that I may restrain all my desires, bringing them into subjection in all things to Your holy will—Amen.   *Treasury of Devotion, 1869*

Good Father, help me not to judge my neighbor. I cannot condone what my neighbor does at times but I can never judge his motives. I find this difficult to do, Lord Father. When I see someone do something wrong I immediately condemn him. How can I condemn his sin and love him as a person? It is only when I look at You, Lord Father, that I have the light and courage to love the sinner and hate his sin—to correct his fault and not judge his motive—to extend forgiveness and forget his offense. Teach me how to stand tall for what is right and not feel any antipathy for those who do not keep Your Law. Give me patience to endure the faults of others, give them the benefit of the doubt and love them with the same merciful compassion You have for them.   *Mother Angelica*

Forgive instantly.
Forgive easily.
Forgive wholeheartedly.
We who have received so much mercy from the Lord
    for our many sins should not withhold but rather
    bestow mercy on those who hurt us.
If God is merciful to us, what right have we
    to deny others of mercy and forgiveness?

There is grace to forgive.
The Lord gives us power to do it.   *Anonymous*

The saints had no hatred, no bitterness. They forgive
everything and think they deserve much more for their
offenses against God.   *St. John Vianney*

FIVE

Knowing Your Father

I cry aloud to the LORD,
   and he answers me from his holy hill.
I lie down and sleep,
   I wake again, for the LORD sustains me.
                                    Psalm 3:4-5

These all look to thee,
   to give them their food in due season.
When thou givest to them, they gather it up;
   when thou openest thy hand,
   they are filled with good things.
When thou hidest thy face, they are dismayed;
   when thou takest away their breath, they die
   and return to their dust.
When thou sendest forth thy Spirit,
   they are created;
   and thou renewest the face of the ground.
                                    Psalm 104:27-30

I appealed to the Lord, the Father of my lord,
   not to forsake me in the days of affliction,

at the time when there is no help
 against the proud.
I will praise thy name continually,
 will sing praise with thanksgiving.
My prayer was heard,
 for thou didst save me from destruction
 and rescue me from an evil plight.
Therefore I will give thanks to thee
 and praise thee,
 and I will bless the name of the Lord.

Sirach 51:10-12

"And I tell you, Ask, and it will be given you; seek, and
you will find; knock, and it will be opened to you. For
every one who asks receives, and he who seeks finds,
and to him who knocks it will be opened. What father
among you, if his son asks for a fish, will instead of a fish
give him a serpent; or if he asks for an egg, will give him
a scorpion? If you then, who are evil, know how to give
good gifts to your children, how much more will the
heavenly Father give the Holy Spirit to those who ask
him!" *Luke 11:9-13*

O gracious and Holy Father, give us wisdom to
perceive you, diligence to seek you, patience to wait for
you, eyes to behold you, a heart to meditate upon you,
and a life to proclaim you; through the power of the
Spirit of Jesus Christ our Lord. *St. Benedict*

Lord, I know not what I ought to ask of You; You only know what I need; You love me better than I know how to love myself. O Father! give to Your child that which he himself knows not how to ask. I dare not ask either for crosses or consolations; I simply present myself before You, I open my heart to You. Behold my needs which I know not myself; see and do according to Your tender mercy. Smite, or heal; depress me, or raise me up; I adore all Your purposes without knowing them; I am silent; I offer myself in sacrifice; I yield myself to You; I would have no other desire than to accomplish Your will. Teach me to pray. Pray Yourself in me— Amen.   *Francois Fénélon*

O God Omnipotent, Who so cares for every one of us, as if You care for him alone; and so for all, as if all were but one! Blessed is the man who loves You, and his friend in You, and his enemy for You. For he only loses none dear to him, to whom all are dear in Him who cannot be lost. And who is that but our God, the God that made heaven and earth, and fills them, even by filling them creating them. And Your law is truth, and truth is Yourself. I behold how some things pass away that others may replace them, but You never depart, O God, my Father supremely good, Beauty of all things beautiful. To You will I entrust whatsoever I have received from You, so shall I lose nothing. Thou made me for Yourself and my heart is restless until it rests in You— Amen.   *St. Augustine of Hippo*

O Heavenly Father, Who watches always over your faithful people, and mightily defends them, so that they be harmless preserved, I most heartily thank You, that it has pleased Your fatherly goodness to take care of me this night past. I most heartily beseech You, O most merciful Father, to show the like kindness toward me this day in preserving my body and soul; that I may neither think, breathe, speak, or do anything that may be displeasing to Your fatherly goodness, dangerous to myself, or hurtful to my neighbor; but that all my doings may be agreeable to Your most blessed will, which is always good; that they may advance Your glory, answer to my vocation, and profit my neighbor, whom I ought to love as myself; that, when You call me hence, I may be found the child not of darkness but of light; through Jesus Christ our Lord—Amen.

Thomas Becon

Do not fear
   what may happen to you tomorrow.
The same Father
   who cares for you today,
   will care for you tomorrow
   and every other day.
Either He will shield you from suffering
   or He will give you unfailing strength
   to bear it.
Be at peace, then,
   and put aside all

anxious thoughts
and imaginings.   *St. Francis de Sales*

The Christian prays in every situation, in his walks for recreation, in his dealings with others, in silence, in reading, in all rational pursuits. And although he is only thinking of God in the little chamber of the soul, and calling upon his father with silent aspirations, God is near him and with him while he is yet speaking.

St. Clement of Alexandria

SIX

Serving Those in Need

Who is like the LORD, our God, who is seated on high,
   who looks far down
   upon the heavens and the earth?
He raises the poor from the dust;
   and lifts the needy from the ash heap,
to make them sit with princes,
   with the princes of his people.
He gives the barren woman a home,
   making her the joyous mother of children.

Psalm 113:5-9

Happy is he whose help is the God of Jacob,
   whose hope is in the LORD his God,
who made heaven and earth,
   the sea, and all that is in them;
who keeps faith for ever;
   who executes justice for the oppressed;
   who gives food to the hungry.

The LORD sets the prisoners free;
    the LORD opens the eyes of the blind.
The LORD lifts up those who are bowed down;
    the LORD loves the righteous.
The LORD watches over the sojourners,
    he upholds the widow and the fatherless;
    but the way of the wicked he brings to ruin.
The LORD will reign for ever,
    thy God, O Zion, to all generations.
Praise the LORD!   *Psalm 146:5-10*

"Then the King will say to those at his right hand,
'Come, O blessed of my Father, inherit the kingdom
prepared for you from the foundation of the world; for I
was hungry and you gave me food, I was thirsty and
you gave me drink, I was a stranger and you welcomed
me, I was naked and you clothed me, I was sick and you
visited me, I was in prison and you came to me.' Then
the righteous will answer him, 'Lord, when did we see
thee hungry and feed thee, or thirsty and give thee
drink? And when did we see thee a stranger and
welcome thee or naked and clothe thee? And when did
we see thee sick or in prison and visit thee?' And the
King will answer them, 'Truly, I say to you, as you did it
to one of the least of these my brethren, you did it to
me.' "   *Matthew 25:34-40*

And Jesus went about all the cities and villages,
teaching in their synagogues and preaching the gospel
of the kingdom, and healing every disease and every

infirmity. When he saw the crowds, he had compassion for them, because they were harassed and helpless like sheep without a shepherd. Then he said to his disciples, "The harvest is plentiful, but the laborers are few; pray therefore the Lord of the harvest to send out laborers into his harvest." *Matthew 9:35-38*

Dear Jesus,
Help us to spread your fragrance everywhere we go.
Flood our souls with your spirit and life.
Penetrate and possess our whole being so utterly
   that our lives may only be a radiance of yours.
Shine through us
and be so in us
that every soul we come in contact with
   may feel your presence in our soul.
Let them look up and see no longer us
but only Jesus.
Stay with us
and then we shall begin to shine as you shine,
so to shine as to be light to others.
The light, O Jesus, will be all from you.
None of it will be ours.
It will be you shining on others through us.
Let us thus praise you in the way you love best
   by shining on those around us.
Let us preach you without preaching
   not by words, but by our example
   by the catching force

the sympathetic influence of what we do
the evident fullness of the love our hearts bear to you.
Amen.   *Mother Teresa of Calcutta*

God, whose mercy and compassion never fail, look
kindly upon the sufferings of all mankind: the needs of
the homeless; the anxieties of prisoners; the pains of the
sick and the injured; the sorrows of the bereaved; the
helplessness of the aged and weak. Comfort and
strengthen them for the sake of your Son, our Saviour
Jesus Christ.   *St. Anselm of Canterbury*

Lord Jesus, when you were on earth, they brought the
sick to you and you healed them all. Today we ask you
to bless all those in sickness, in weakness and in pain;

Those who are blind and who cannot see the light of
    the sun;
    the beauty of the world, or the faces of their friends;
    those who are deaf and cannot hear the voices which
      speak to them;
    those who are helpless and who must lie in bed while
      others go out and in.
Bless all such.
Those whose minds have lost their reason;
those who are so nervous that they cannot cope with
    life;
those who worry about everything.
Bless all such.
Those who must face life under some handicap;

those whose weakness means that they must always
    be careful;
those who are lame and maimed and cannot enter into
    any of
  the strenuous activities or pleasures of life.
Bless all such.

Grant that we in our health and our strength may never
find those who are weak and handicapped a nuisance,
but grant that we may always do and give all that we
can to help them, and to make life easier for them.

O Lord, do not let us turn into "broken cisterns," that
can hold no water. Do not let us be so blinded by the
enjoyment of the good things of earth that our hearts
become insensitive to the cry of the poor, of the sick, of
orphaned children and of those innumerable brothers
of ours who lack the necessary minimum to eat, to
clothe their nakedness, and to gather their family
together under one roof.   *Pope John XXIII*

Give us patience and fortitude to put self aside for you
in the most unlikely people; to know that every man's
and any man's suffering is our own first business, for
which we must be willing to go out of our way and to
leave our own interests.   *Caryll Houselander*

Father, lover of life, we pray for those suffering from
disease for which, at present, there is no known cure;
give them confidence in your love and never-failing

support and a stronger faith in the resurrection. Grant wisdom and perseverance to all working to discover the causes of the disease, so that they see in their labours the ministry of your Son, who himself showed forth his divine power by healing those who came to him.   *George Appleton*

Lord, have mercy.
Restore me to liberty
and enable me to so live now
that I may answer before thee and before men.
Lord, whatever this day may bring,
thy name be praised.
Amen.
Dietrich Bonhoeffer (1906-1945)

At the end of life we will not be judged by
    how many diplomas we have received
    how much money we have made
    how many great things we have done.
We will be judged by
    "I was hungry and you gave me to eat
    I was naked and you clothed me
    I was homeless and you took me in."
Hungry not only for bread
    —but hungry for love
Naked not only for clothing
    —but naked of human dignity and respect
Homeless not only for want of a room of bricks

—but homeless because of rejection.
This is Christ in distressing disguise.

Mother Teresa of Calcutta

Christ has no body now on earth but yours, no hands but yours, no feet but yours; yours are the eyes through which Christ's compassion looks out on the world, yours are the feet with which he is to go about doing good, and yours are the hands with which he is to bless us now.   *St. Teresa of Avila*

SEVEN

Strength for Today

I rise before dawn and cry for help;
  I hope in thy words.
My eyes are awake before the watches of the night,
  that I may meditate upon thy promise.
                    Psalm 119:147-148

A Song of Ascents.
I lift up my eyes to the hills.
  From whence does my help come?
My help comes from the LORD,
  who made heaven and earth.
He will not let your foot be moved,
  he who keeps you will not slumber.
Behold, he who keeps Israel
  will neither slumber nor sleep.
The LORD is your keeper;
  the LORD is your shade
  on your right hand.
The sun shall not smite you by day,
  nor the moon by night.

The LORD will guard you from all evil;
  he will keep your life.
The LORD will keep
  your going out and your coming in
  from this time forth and for evermore.
Psalm 121

But I will sing of thy might;
I will sing aloud of they steadfast love in the morning.
For thou hast been to me a fortress
  and a refuge in the day of my distress.
O my strength, I will sing praises to thee,
  for thou, O God, art my fortress,
  the God who shows me steadfast love.
Psalm 59:16-17

But this I call to mind,
  and therefore I have hope:
The steadfast love of the LORD never ceases,
  his mercies never come to an end;
they are new every morning;
  great is thy faithfulness.
"The LORD is my portion," says my soul;
  "therefore I will hope in him." *Lamentations 3:21-24*

O Merciful God, be Thou now unto me a strong tower of defence, I humbly entreat Thee. Give me grace to await Thy leisure, and patiently to bear what Thou doest unto me; nothing doubting or mistrusting Thy goodness towards me; for Thou knowest what is good for me better than I do. Therefore, do with me in all things what Thou wilt; only arm me, I beseech Thee, with Thine armor, that I may stand fast; above all things, taking to me the shield of faith; praying always that I may refer myself wholly to Thy will, abiding Thy pleasure, and comforting myself in those troubles which it shall please Thee to send me, seeing such troubles are profitable for me; and I am assuredly persuaded that all Thou doest cannot but be well; and unto Thee be all honor and glory—Amen.   *Lady Jane Grey*

When the dawn appears,
When the light grows,
When midday burns,
When has ceased the holy light,
When the clear night comes;
I sing your praises, O Father,
Healer of hearts,
Healer of bodies,
Giver of wisdom,
Remedy of evil.   *Synesius of Cyrene*

Lord, may I be wakeful at sunrise to begin a new day for you; cheerful at sunset for having done my work for you; thankful at moonrise and under starshine for the beauty of your universe. And may I add what little may be in me to add to your great world.   *The Abbot of Greve*

As I begin this day
become flesh again
in me, Father.
Let your timeless and everlasting love
live out this sunrise to sunset
within the possibilities,
and the impossibilities
of my own, very human life.
Help me to become
Christ to my neighbor,
food to the hungry,
health to the sick,
friend to the lonely,
freedom to the enslaved,
in all my daily living.   *J. Barrie Shepherd*

Into your hands, O Lord, we commend ourselves this day. Let your presence be with us to its close. Strengthen us to remember that in whatsoever good work we do we are serving you. Give us a diligent and watchful spirit, that we may seek in all things to know your will, and knowing it, gladly to perform it, to the honour and glory of your name; through Jesus Christ our Lord.   *Gelasian Sacramentary*

Be patient with every one, but above all with yourself. I mean, do not be disturbed because of your imperfections, and always rise up bravely from a fall. I am glad that you daily make a new beginning; there is no better means of progress in the spiritual life than to be continually beginning afresh, and never to think that we have done enough.   *St. Francis de Sales*

Cheered by the presence of God, I will do each moment, without anxiety, according to the strength which He shall give me, the work which his providence assigns me.   *Francois Fénélon*

Once sacrificed life's loveliness for me—
I thank Thee, God, that I have lived.

Elizabeth, Countess of Craven

Thanks be to thee,
my joy and my glory
and my hope and my God.
Thanks be to thee for thy gifts;
but do thou preserve them in me,
thus thou wilt preserve me,
and the things thou hast given me
will increase and be made perfect,
and I shall be with thee:
because even that I exist is thy gift. *St. Augustine of Hippo*

My God, from my heart I thank you for the many
blessings you have given me. I thank you for having
created and baptised me, for having placed me in your
holy Church, and for having given me so many graces
and mercies through the merits of Jesus Christ. I thank
your Son Jesus, for having died upon the cross that I
might receive pardon for my sins and obtain my eternal
salvation. I thank you for all your other mercies you
have given me through Jesus Christ, Our Lord.

Michael Buckley

Lord, renew our spirits and draw our hearts to Yourself,
that our work may not be to us a burden, but a delight,

and give us such a mighty love for You as may sweeten all our obedience. Oh, let us not serve You with the spirit of bondage as slaves, but with cheerfulness and gladness of children, delighting ourselves in you and rejoicing in your work. Amen.   *Rev. Benjamin Jenks*

Kind Jesus, You promised me Joy—the kind of Joy no-one can take away. You told Your Apostles that You bequeathed joy to all of us and yet so few people possess joy. I find myself in a quandary at times because somehow I feel my lack of joy is my own fault. Is it because the joy I seek is emotional, with its source in people and things of this world? If this is the reason, then certainly my joy would be short-lived. Is it because I desire to please myself in everything and since it is impossible for things to go my way, my joy is tucked away in some corner until all is well again? Perhaps I think joy is happiness—that exuberant feeling that comes over me when exterior things please me. I have forgotten what joy is, my Lord. I find it difficult to remember that it is possible to have joy in sorrow, joy in pain and joy in disappointments. Teach me, my Jesus, how to maintain joy in the midst of difficulties, the kind of joy that is the fruit of Your Presence in my soul, Your love in my heart, the joy that comes from a loving acceptance of the Father's Will in my moment to moment existence. To know that whatever happens to me has first passed through His Divine Mind would be a source of joy. To realize that

He will bring good out of every injustice and every heartache will calm my soul so joy may blossom in the midst of trial and tragedy. Yes, my Lord, give me the joy that will never be lessened by the things of this world because it is rooted in your love and Your Presence.

Mother Angelica

Dear Jesus, most of the time it is easier to talk to you about my sorrows than my joys because I am often more aware of pain and unhappiness. But I realize that you promised to give me your own joy to flood my being with new life. Forgive me for the times I fail to appropriate this gift and prefer to wallow in negativity. I believe you want me to be happy because "the joy of the Lord is my strength." Give me courage and confidence to continue the journey of faith. Thank you for this marvelous gift of joy which renews my spirit and brings hope for the future.   *Barbara Shlemon*

Today my heart sings, Lord;
Everything within me rejoices.
Joy bubbles up in my soul,
overflows and cascades like a stream leaping all
     barriers;
the joy of knowing You,
the joy of union with You.
One with You, Creator of the world,
and my Creator,
one with You, Saviour of the world,

and my Saviour.
One with You, Spirit of the eternal God,
and my God,
one with You, almighty King of kings
and my Lord and King.
Joy, joy at the heart of living,
joy in doing, joy in being;
sing for joy, my heart,
for sheer joy, my soul.
The joy of loving You,
the joy of following You,
the joy of serving You;
all the way 'long it is glory.
Today my heart sings, Lord;
everything within me rejoices,
joy bubbles up in my soul,
glory . . . glory!   *Flora Larsson*

O Tender Father,
You gave me more, much more than I ever thought to
ask for. I realize that our human desires can never really
match what you long to give us.
Thanks, and again thanks, O Father, for having granted
my petitions, and that which I never realized I needed
or petitioned. Amen.   *St. Catherine of Siena*

Christ came to bring joy: joy to children, joy to parents,
joy to families and to friends, joy to workers and to

scholars, joy to the sick and to the elderly, joy to all humanity. In a true sense, joy is the keynote of the Christian message. . . .

We are an Easter people and "Alleluia" is our song. With St. Paul I exhort you: "Rejoice in the Lord always, I say it again, rejoice" (Phil 4:4).
Rejoice because Jesus has come into the world!
Rejoice because Jesus has died upon the cross!
Rejoice because he rose from the dead!
Rejoice because in baptism he washed away our sins!
Rejoice because Jesus has come to set us free!
And rejoice because he is the Master of our life!

Pope John Paul II

So abandon yourself utterly for the love of God, and in this way you will become truly happy.   *Blessed Henry Suso*

It is always springtime in the heart that loves God.

St. John Vianney

NINE

Letting God's Kingdom Come

The prayer was to this effect: "O Lord, Lord God, Creator of all things, Who art awe-inspiring and strong and just and merciful, who alone art King and art kind, who alone art bountiful, who alone art just and almighty and eternal, who dost rescue Israel from every evil, who didst choose the fathers and consecrate them; accept this sacrifice on behalf of all thy people Israel and preserve thy portion and make it holy. Gather together our scattered people, set free those who are slaves among the Gentiles, look upon those who are rejected and despised, and let the Gentiles know that thou art our God.   *2 Maccabees 1:24-27*

Therefore David blessed the LORD in the presence of all the assembly; and David said: "Blessed art thou, O LORD, the God of Israel our father, for ever and ever. Thine, O LORD, is the greatness, and the power, and the glory, and the victory, and the majesty; for all that is in the heavens and in the earth is thine; thine is the kingdom O LORD, and thou art exalted as head above all. Both riches and honor come from thee, and thou rulest over all. In thy hand are power and might; and in thy hand it is to make great and to give strength to all. And now we thank thee, our God, and praise thy glorious name." *1 Chronicles 29:10-13*

And he said to his disciples, "Therefore I tell you, do not be anxious about your life, what you will eat, nor about your body, what you shall put on. For life is more than food, and the body more than clothing. Consider the ravens: they neither sow nor reap, they have neither storehouse nor barn, and yet God feeds them. Of how much more value are you than the birds! And which of you by being anxious can add a cubit to his span of life? If then you are not able to do as small a thing as that, why are you anxious about the rest? Consider the lilies, how they grow; they neither toil nor spin. Yet I tell you, even Solomon in all his glory was not arrayed like one of these. But if God so clothes the grass which is alive in the field today and tomorrow is thrown into the oven, how much more will he clothe you, O men of little faith? And do not seek what you are to eat and what you are to drink, nor be of anxious mind. For all the nations of the world seek these things; and your Father knows that you need them. Instead, seek his kingdom, and these things shall be yours as well. "Fear not, little flock, for it is your Father's good pleasure to give you

the kingdom. Sell your possessions, and give alms;
provide yourselves with purses that do not grow old,
with a treasure in the heavens that does not fail, where
no thief approaches and no moth destroys. For where
your treasure is, there will your heart be also."

Luke 12:22-34

"Pray then like this:
Our Father who art in heaven,
   Hallowed be thy name,
   Thy kingdom come,
   Thy will be done,
   On earth as it is in heaven.
   Give us this day our daily bread;
And forgive us our debts,
   As we also have forgiven our debtors;
And lead us not into temptation,
   But deliver us from evil." *Matthew 6:9-13*

O God, our Leader and our Master and our Friend,
forgive our imperfections and our little motives, take us
and make us one with Thy great purpose, use us and do
not reject us, make us all servants of Thy kingdom,
weave our lives into Thy struggle to conquer and to
bring peace and union to the world.

We are small and feeble creatures, we are feeble in
speech, feebler still in action, nevertheless let but Thy
light shine upon us, and there is not one of us who
cannot be lit by Thy fire and who cannot lose himself in

Thy salvation. Take us into Thy purposes, O God. Let Thy kingdom come into our hearts and into this world.

H.G. Wells

Make us receptive and open
and may we accept your kingdom
like children taking bread
from the hands of their father.
Let us live in your peace,
at home with you
all the days of our lives.   *Huub Oosterhuis*

O God of all the nations of the earth, remember those who, though created in your image, are ignorant of your love; and, in fulfillment of the sacrifice of your Son Jesus Christ, let the prayers and labours of your Church deliver them from false faith and unbelief, and bring them to worship you; through him who is the resurrection and the life of all who put their trust in you, Jesus Christ our Lord.   *St. Francis Xavier*

O Lord, who though thou was rich yet for our sakes didst become poor, and hast promised in thy holy gospel that whatsoever is done to the least of thy brethren thou wilt receive as done to thee: Give us grace, we humbly beseech thee, to be ever willing and ready to minister, as thou enablest us, to the needs of others, and to extend the blessings of thy kingdom over all the world; to thy praise and glory, who art God over all, blessed for ever.   *St. Augustine of Hippo*

O Lord, who has set before us the great hope that thy kingdom shall come on earth, and hast taught us to pray for its coming: Give us grace to discern the signs of its dawning, and to work for the perfect day when thy will shall be done on earth as it is in heaven; through Jesus Christ our Lord.   *Percy Dearmer*

Resolve henceforth to keep Heaven before your mind, to be ready to forego everything that can hinder you or cause you to stray in your journey there.

St. Francis de Sales

Brief life is here our portion,
   Brief sorrow, short-lived care:
The life that knows no ending,
   The tearless life, is there.
O happy retribution:
   Short toil, eternal rest;
For mortals and for sinners
   A mansion with the blest!
And now we fight the battle,
   But then shall wear the crown
Of full and everlasting
   And passionless renown,
And now we watch and struggle,

And now we live in hope,
And Sion in her anguish
    With Babylon must cope.
But he whom now we trust in
    Shall then be seen and known,
And they that know and see him
    Shall have him for their own.
The morning shall awaken,
    The shadows shall decay,
And each true-hearted servant
    Shall shine as doth the day.
There God, our King and portion,
    In fulness of his grace,
Shall we behold for ever,
    And worship face to face.
Then all the halls of Sion
    For ay shall be complete
And in the Land of Beauty
    All things of beauty meet.   *Bernard of Cluny*

O sweet and blessed country,
    The home of God's elect!
O sweet and blessed country
    That eager hearts expect!
Jesu, in mercy bring us
    To that dear land of rest;
Who art, with God the Father
    And Spirit, ever blest.   *Bernard of Cluny*

Mary: The Christian Model of Womanhood

And when they met her they all blessed her with one accord and said to her,
"You are the exaltation of Jerusalem,
 You are the great glory of Israel,
 you are the great pride of our nation!
You have done all this singlehanded;
 you have done great good to Israel,
 and God is well pleased with it.
May the Almighty Lord bless you
 for ever!"
And all the people said "So be it!" *Judith 15:9-10*

Therefore the Lord himself will give you a sign. Behold, a young woman shall conceive and bear a son, and shall call his name Immanuel. *Isaiah 7:14*

And Mary said,
"My soul magnifies the Lord,

and my spirit rejoices in God my Savior,
for he has regarded the low estate of his handmaiden.
For behold, henceforth all generations will call me
blessed;
for he who is mighty has done great things for me,
and holy is his name.
And his mercy is on those who fear him
from generation to generation.
He has shown strength with his arm,
he has scattered the proud in the imagination of their
hearts,
he has put down the mighty from their thrones,
and exalted those of low degree.
he has filled the hungry with good things,
and the rich he has sent empty away.
He has helped his servant Israel,
in remembrance of his mercy,
as he spoke to our fathers,
to Abraham and to his posterity for ever.'' *Luke 1:46-55*

By you we have access to your Son, O blessed finder of
grace, Mother of Life, Mother of Salvation, that by you
He may receive us, Who by you was given to us.

St. Bernard of Clairvaux

O you who are full of grace, all creation rejoices in you!
The hierarchies of the angels and the race of men
rejoice. O sanctified temple and rational paradise,
virginal glory, of whom God took flesh! He Who is God

before all ages, became a child. Your womb He made His throne, and your lap He made greater than the heavens. Indeed all creation exults in you. Glory be to you! *From the Byzantine Liturgy of St. Basil*

Holy Virgin Mary, there is none like you born in the world among women. O daughter and handmaid of the most High King, the heavenly Father! Mother of our Most High Lord Jesus Christ! Spouse of the Holy Ghost! Pray for us . . . to your most holy Son, our Lord and Master. *St. Francis of Assisi*

O my Lady, Holy Mary, hope of all Christians, Queen of Angels and of all of God's Saints in Heaven.

St. Francis Xavier

How happy my soul was, good Mother,
when I had the good fortune to gaze upon you!
How I love to recall the pleasant moments spent
under your gaze, so full of kindness and mercy for us.
Yes, tender Mother, you stooped down to earth
to appear to a mere child . . . You, the Queen
of heaven and earth, deigned to make use
of the most fragile thing in the world's eyes.

St. Bernadette

Hers was the hidden treasure of modesty, hers the self sacrifice of earnestness, hers to be the pattern of maidenhood at home, of kinswomanhood in ministry, of motherhood in the temple. O how many virgins has she presented to the Lord, saying: "Here is one who (like me) has kept stainlessly clean the wedding chamber." *St. Ambrose*

If you look diligently at Mary, there is nothing of virtue, nothing of beauty, nothing of splendor or glory which does not shine in her. *St. Jerome*

The knot tied by Eve's disobedience, was untied by the obedience of Mary. *St. Irenaeus*

When Mary Immaculate, the finest and most fragrant flower of all creation said in answer to the angel's greeting: "Behold the handmaid of the Lord," she accepted the honor of divine motherhood, which was in that moment realized within her. And we, born once in our father Adam, formerly the adopted sons of God but fallen from that high estate, are now once more brothers, adopted sons of the Father, restored to his adoption by the redemption which has already begun. At the foot of the Cross, we shall be the children of Mary, with that same Jesus whom she conceived at the Annunciation. From today onwards, she will be the Mother of God and our Mother too. *Pope John XXIII*

Part II

Lord, Walk with Me Today

ONE

Grace for Busy Times

Blessed be the Lord,
   who daily bears us up;
   God is our salvation.   *Psalm 68:19*

I set the LORD always before me;
   because he is at my right hand,
   I shall not be moved.   *Psalm 16:8*

Let not loyalty and faithfulness forsake you;
   bind them about your neck,
   write them on the tablet of your heart.
So you will find favor and good repute
   in the sight of God and man.
Trust in the LORD with all your heart,
   and do not rely on your own insight.
In all your ways acknowledge him,
   and he will make straight your paths.   *Proverbs 3:3-6*

Slow me down Lord,
ease the pounding of my heart

by the quieting of my mind.
Teach me the art of slowing down,
to look at a flower,
to chat to a friend,
to read a few lines from a good book.
Remind me each day of the fable
of the hare and the tortoise,
that I may know that the race
is not always to the swift,
that there is more to life than
increasing its speed.
Let me look upward into the
branches of the towering oak
and know that it grew great and
strong because it grew slowly
and well.
Slow me down, Lord, and inspire
me to send my roots deep into
the soil of life's enduring
values that I may grow toward
the stars of my greater destiny.

Calm me down, Lord, with your presence.
Open my heart to the smooth flowing
    of your serene spirit.
I am grateful to find this calm moment
    in your presence.
For I have been too excited,
    too busy with many activities.

I want to rest, Lord, in the shade
  of your power and love.
Restore my strength as only you know how.
Lord, I entered the battle with all my heart,
  and did not shrink from helping others
  who needed me.
Your kindness now rests on me
  like the pacifying blessing I have been yearning for.
No disquiet stirs in me,
  because you lead me to the sweet repose
  of a clear and quiet conscience.
I try to fulfill my part in creation
  and in the harmony of life.
Lord, overshadow me with your blessing.
Working side by side with my brothers and sisters
  for a better world,
  I find the meaning of my life.
Give me the opportunity to soothe my spirit.
I take refuge in you, Lord. Amen.   *Hugo Schlesinger*
                                     Humberto Porto

O Lord, thou knowest how busy I must be this day;
if I forget thee, do not thou forget me.   *Sir Jacob Astley*

May the Lord support us all the day long, till the shades
lengthen and the evening comes, and the busy world is
hushed, and the fever of life is over, and our work is
done. Then in his mercy, may he give us a safe lodging

and a holy rest, and peace at the last. Father, we ask this through Jesus Christ our Lord.   *John Henry Cardinal Newman*

My candle burns at both ends, Lord—and that makes it hard to find a candlestick!

I love the flame of excitement in today's fast-paced life-style. I delight in the bright light of all the possibilities, all the sights to see, all the doors to open. I bask in the warmth of the opportunity to have a home, a family, a career, hobbies, continuing education, travel, and fun, too.

But I still have only a 24-hour day, Lord. I know I can't be all things to all people. I can't even be all things to myself. My candle has been burning too brightly for me to be able to get a hold on it. Help me, Lord. Light my way. Show me which parts of my life I should keep burning brightly and which ones I should snuff out.

Help me to center my dreams and goals and shining hopes on you, Lord, and never lose sight of your burning love that is the beacon to guide me, the warmth to cheer me, and the flame to light up my life.

Bernadette McCarver Snyder

"Child of My love, lean hard,
And let Me feel the pressure of thy care;
I know thy burden, child. I shaped it;
Poised it in Mine Own hand; made no proportion
In its weight to thine unaided strength,

For even as I laid it on, I said,
'I shall be near, and while she leans on Me,
This burden shall be Mine, not hers;
so shall I keep My child within the circling arms
Of My Own love.' Here lay it down, nor fear
To impose it on a shoulder which upholds
The government of worlds. Yet closer come:
Thou art not near enough. I would embrace thy care;
So I might feel My child reposing on My breast.
Thou lovest Me? I knew it. Doubt not then;
But loving Me, lean hard.''   *Anonymous*

TWO

Time Out for God

I keep the LORD always before me;
  because he is at my right hand, I shall not be moved.
Therefore my heart is glad, and my soul rejoices;
  my body also dwells secure.
For thou dost not give me up to Sheol,
  or let thy godly one see the pit.
Thou dost show me the path of life;
  in thy presence there is fulness of joy,
  in thy right hand are pleasures for evermore.
Psalm 16:8-11

It is good to give thanks to the LORD,
  to sing praise to thy name, O Most High;
to declare thy steadfast love in the morning,
  and thy faithfulness by night,
to the music of the lute and the harp,
  to the melody of the lyre.
For thou, O LORD, hast made me glad by thy work;
  at the works of thy hands I sing for joy. *Psalm 92:1-4*

Now as they went on their way, he entered a village;
and a woman named Martha received him into her
house. And she had a sister called Mary, who sat at the
Lord's feet and listened to his teaching. But Martha was
distracted with much serving; and she went to him and
said, "Lord, do you not care that my sister has left me to
serve alone? Tell her then to help me." But the Lord
answered her, "Martha, Martha, you are anxious and
troubled about many things; one thing is needful. Mary
has chosen the good portion, which shall not be taken
away from her."   *Luke 10:38-42*

As I begin this day
become flesh again
in me, Father.
Let your timeless and everlasting love
live out this sunrise to sunset
within the possibilities,
and the impossibilities
of my own, very human life.
Help me to become
Christ to my neighbour,
food to the hungry,
health to the sick,
friend to the lonely,
freedom to the enslaved,
in all my daily living.   *J. Barrie Shepherd*

In meditation let the person rouse himself from things
temporal, and let him collect himself within himself—

that is to say, within the very center of his soul, where lies impressed the very image of God. Here let him hearken to the voice of God as though speaking to him from on high, yet present in his soul, as though there were no other voice in the world save God and himself.

San Pedro de Alcantara

I am tired, Lord,
too tired to think,
too tired to pray,
too tired to do anything.
Too tired,
drained of resources,
"labouring at the oars against a head wind,"
pressed down by a force as strong as the sea.
Lord of all power and might,
"your way was through the sea,
your path through the great waters,"
calm my soul,
take control,
Lord of all power and might.   *Rex Chapman*

The Christian prays in every situation, in his walks for recreation, in his dealings with others, in silence, in reading, in all rational pursuits. And although he is only thinking of God in the little chamber of the soul, and calling upon his Father with silent aspirations, God is near him and with him while he is yet speaking.

St. Clement of Alexandria

THREE

Offering Your Work to God

Satisfy us in the morning with thy steadfast love,
   that we may rejoice and be glad all our days.
Make us glad as many days as thou hast afflicted us,
   and as many years as we have seen evil.
Let thy work be manifest to thy servants,
   and thy glorious power to their children.
Let the favor of the Lord our God be upon us,
   and establish thou the work of our hands upon us,
   Yea, the work of our hands establish thou it.
                                        Psalm 90:14-17

Commit your work to the LORD,
   and your plans will be established.   *Proverbs 16:3*

O Lord God, the Almighty who gives strength to the
weak, conscious that I can do nothing without your
help, I pray for your gracious assistance in all my duties.
I come to you, Lord of all power and love, trusting

completely that you will supply what is wanting in me.
My God, may your grace be sufficient for me and
always with me that I may do everything faithfully and
well, through Jesus Christ. Amen. *Benjamin Jenks*

Father, light up the small duties of this day's life; may
they shine with the beauty of Thy countenance. May
we believe that glory may dwell in the commonest task
of every day. *St. Augustine*

O God, give me strength today for anything that is hard
to face or difficult to do;
  Give me enthusiasm to share with others the tasks
that we shall do together;
  Give me integrity and unselfishness, that the reward
may be fairly shared;
  Give me humility when things go exceptionally well
and patience when results are long in coming.
If I am subject to criticism, help me to take it well;
  Show me where I can do better;
  Show me where another could develop new strengths
if he could have more help from me;
  Show me where a little humour would help when
spirits are ruffled and tired. So let us serve you and
those who depend on us. *Rita Snowden*

For life, and health, and all good gifts, I bring my
thanks, O God, at the day's beginning.
  Bless the intimate relationships of my home this day

and let me show love and gentleness and good cheer.
  Save me from being touchy;
  Save me from stubbornness in any situation;
  Save from impatience.
Apart from my own interests, let me spare time for the interests of others;
Apart from my own ideas, let me show tolerance for the ideas of others;
Apart from my own earnings and use of money, let me be aware of the needs of others.
  Let the sacredness of persons be very real to me:
  Let the tyranny of things not overwhelm me;
  Let the lasting truth and goodness and beauty of your kingdom have first place in all my plans. Amen.

Rita Snowden

Lord Jesus, you know that my work as a homemaker can be very tiring and frustrating sometimes. Forgive me for the times when I grumble and complain about the many things I need to do each day.
  Lord, you know that I do love to serve my family well. I want to do my chores with gladness of heart. I offer my work to you this day, Lord. Refresh my vision for it. Grant me the ability to become more organized. Grant me the strength to perform my responsibilities. Make me serve my family with joy! Amen. *Anonymous*

My Jesus, how often I feel very small and inadequate before great tasks and responsibilities. What can I do but bring all that I have, even though it isn't much, and place all this in Your hands, wait for Your blessing, breaking, thanking and receive back again with amazing power to reach all who depend on me, fill them with goodness and still have more than what I started with. May I never hold back my gifts from You. May I believe that Your blessing multiplies my smallest gifts to maximum powers. May I rejoice that You return the task to me and I have the personal thrill of seeing many satisfied by my ministrations. I adore Your wisdom, Your power, Your sharing. Amen.

Father Gerald Keefe

Lord Jesus,
   I give you my hands to do your work.
   I give you my feet to go your way.
   I give you my eyes to see as you do.
   I give you my tongue to speak your words.
   I give you my mind that you may think in me.
   I give you my spirit that you may pray in me.
Above all,
   I give you my heart that you may love in me,
   your Father, and all mankind.
   I give you my whole self that you may grow in me,
   so that it is you, Lord Jesus.
   who live and work and pray in me.   *The Grail*

"Sing unto the Lord!"
Even on the days which are loaded with work?

Yes, especially then.
When we sing, we bring heaven down to us.
God inclines Himself to us when we sing praises to Him, and He will fill our work with His Spirit.
Then our work will be blessed and prosperous. And we will become strong enough to tread the difficulties under our feet. Thus our work will bring eternal fruit, because it has been done in God.   *Basilea Schlink*

There is nothing small in the service of God.
St. Francis de Sales

FOUR

Praying for Your Children

Then Raguel blessed God and said,
"Blessed art thou, O God, with every pure and holy blessing.
  Let thy saints and all thy creatures bless thee;
  Let all thy angels and thy chosen people bless thee for ever.
Blessed art thou, because thou hast made me glad.
  It has not happened to me as I expected;
  but thou has treated us according to thy great mercy.
Blessed art thou, because thou hast had compassion on two only children.
  Show them mercy, O Lord;
  and bring their lives to fulfilment in health
  and happiness and mercy." *Tobit 8:15-17*

The LORD bless you and keep you:
The LORD make his face to shine upon

you, and be gracious to you:
The LORD lift up his countenance upon you, and
give you peace.   *Numbers 6:24-26*

Fathers, do not provoke your children to anger, but
bring them up in the discipline and instruction of the
Lord.   *Ephesians 6:4*

Father, I thank you for all my children.
You have given them all to me to love,
care for, and raise for your purposes.
Grant me the grace to love each one of them
the way you want me to love them.
Grant me the faithfulness to take care of all their needs.
Grant me the wisdom to lead them to your plans for
their lives.
Grant me a deep joy for being their mother. Amen.

Anonymous

Heavenly Father, forgive me for my impatience,
unkindness, and selfishness towards my children.
Forgive me for making them meet my own standards
instead of yours.
Teach me, Father, to humbly seek your will for each
one of them.
I surrender to you my plans for their lives.
And Lord, make me patient, kind, and loving towards
them.

Teach me better ways to express my love to them.
Help me, Father. Amen.   *Anonymous*

O Lord, help me.
I am so tired, so tired.
I love this little child,
but I am physically and emotionally worn-out.
Infants are demanding—
late nights,
daybreak mornings,
unpredictable schedules.
And I never dreamed how emotionally unstrung
I would feel.
I don't understand why the baby is crying.
The baby doesn't respond to me as a person.
I'm depressed.
I feel alone.
Calm me, Lord.
This will end soon.
Schedules will emerge.
Baby will sleep longer.
I will be more energetic.
I can find satisfactions
if not in meaningful coos and smiles
then in the warmth of a baby close to me,
needing me.
I can seek relief—
go shopping some evening,

share my feelings with my husband,
call friends who are glad to listen or talk awhile,
call the doctor to ask all my "little" questions,
(I have been too proud to admit I don't know)
and I can snatch
every spare moment of rest possible.
Help me relax as I realize
an infant is more than smiles, rosy cheeks,
and affectionate sounds.
But a child, a new baby, is a miracle—
new, ongoing life in your creation.
Thank you.   *Judith Mattison*

We are worried about our children, Lord.
They seem at times to be rebellious
and indifferent to you and your purposes.
We can't help but feel that we are to blame
when they take off on their precarious journeys
and flirt with those demons of darkness
that are capable of destroying their souls.
We know, O God, that our love for them
cannot coerce them into goodness
any more than your divine and eternal love
can compel us to follow you.
Maybe we are too absorbed in our own failures
and embarrassed by our inability
to lead them aright.
Perhaps our love is selfish—

that we don't love them enough to let them go
even if we can't hold them back.
Help us, O God,
to love them as you love us,
patiently and perpetually,
whatever their decisions and actions.
And, though we cannot program their lives
to fit into our agenda for them,
help us to live in a way
that will lovingly influence them
and eventually draw them back to you.

Leslie and Edith Brandt

Plowing and Planting—that seems to be my whole life, Lord. Every day I keep trying to plow through my son's room, thinking there must be a kid in there somewhere! And I am always trying to plant seeds of caution, of good manners, of clean living, of religious fervor.

The plowing has gotten me nowhere. I can get a furrow made through the piles of smelly socks, school projects, empty root beer bottles, telescopes, microscopes, and dissected frogs—but the next day the path has disappeared and it's time to start plowing again. No matter how hard I try, I have never been able to get that field cleared of debris.

And as I am planting, Lord, I keep thinking, "The kingdom of heaven is like a man who sowed good seed in his field. While the people were sleeping, his enemy came and sowed weeds amidst the harvest and then went away.''

Lord, we try to sow good seeds in our families, and then the enemy comes and sows weeds through TV, movies, rock music lyrics, peer pressure, and even some school programs. Show us what is happening while we are sleeping, Lord. Help us be alert enough to notice when the weeds start growing—and show us a way to weed out the bad influences before it is too late.

The plowing we will have always with us—and I have gotten used to furrowing through the ant farms and the overdue library books and the backpacks still packed with dirty clothes from last week's hike and the footballs, baseballs, and dust balls. But, Lord, I need your help in the planting.

Help me—help us all, Lord—to weed and seed carefully enough so we can cultivate in our children a respect for your teachings and lead them to your rich harvest of love.   *Bernadette McCarver Snyder*

Blessed are you, Lord, Creator of the Universe;
     you give life to human beings.
You created humankind in your image and likeness;
     you breathed in their nostrils
     love for all that lives.
Blessed are you, Lord, Merciful Father;
     You keep within my body
     the wonder of the human seed.

Thus you give life and form
   to my child.
Blessed are you, Lord, holy and kind;
   you allow me to reach the moment of childbirth
   with a steadfast and happy heart.
May the time stipulated by you
   for giving birth
   be an hour of health, peace, and tranquility.
Blessed are you Lord, our King and Savior;
   may the tears of concern and excitement
   bring forth your full blessing for my newborn.
Both of us, mother and baby, remain in your hands.
Blessed are you, Lord, Great and Sovereign God;
   give me the joy to care for my child.
May we live in happiness
   under your constant shining light
   and infinite love.
Amen.   *Humberto Porto*
            Hugo Schlesinger

A baby is on the way, Lord,
and our hearts are filled
with every-increasing delight
as we marvel at the awesome mystery
of being cocreators with you.
We are grateful for this blessed privilege.
Even while we parents-to-be rejoice
in being the recipients of your love
and the instruments of your will,

we regard with apprehension
this responsibility that is ours.
We feel so much
the need of relating more deeply to you.
We look forward with expectancy and joy
to the birth of our child.
As we cling more closely to one another,
we commit ourselves to you
resting in the confidence
that this baby is in your embrace,
that you will care for our child and for us.
We pray that each of us and our child may be
your children
and your beloved servants forever.

Leslie and Edith Brandt

Heavenly Father, from whom all parenthood comes, teach us so to understand our children that they may grow in your wisdom and love according to your holy will. Fill us with sensitive respect for the great gift of human life which you have committed to our care, help us to listen with patience to their worries and problems and give us the tolerance to allow them to develop, as individuals, as your Son did under the loving guidance of Mary and Joseph.   *Michael Buckley*

Father, lover of life and of the human family, who co-operated with me in the birth of my children, be with me now and help me in my task of raising them up as children of your kingdom. May they give you constant praise and adoration and be, to me, a never-ending source of gratitude and thanksgiving.

Michael Buckley

Our children
are not just our children.
They happen to be the Lord's.
They are his first
before they are ours.
The Lord loves them much more than we do.
His plans for them are surely better than ours.
The best way we can raise them up is to see to it
    first that they know and love God, who is their
      true Father.
If they are in God's hands, what have we to fear?

Anonymous

FIVE

Praying for Your Husband

Happy is the husband of a good wife;
  the number of his days will be doubled.
A loyal wife rejoices her husband,
  and he will complete his life in peace.
A good wife is a great blessing;
  she will be granted among the blessings of the man
who fears the Lord.
Whether rich or poor, his heart is glad,
  and at all times his face is cheerful. . . .
A wife's charm delights her husband,
  and her skill puts fat on his bones;
A silent wife is a gift of the Lord,
  and there is nothing so precious as a disciplined soul.
A modest wife adds charm to charm,
  and no balance can weigh the value of a chaste soul.
Like the sun rising in the heights of the Lord,
  so is the beauty of a good wife in her well-ordered
    home.

Like the shining lamp on the holy lampstand,
so is a beautiful face on a stately figure.
Like pillars of gold on a base of silver,
so are beautiful feet with a steadfast heart.

Sirach 26:1-4, 13-18

Be subject to one another out of reverence for Christ. Wives, be subject to your husbands, as to the Lord. For the husband is the head of the wife as Christ is the head of the church, his body, and is himself its Savior. As the church is subject to Christ, so let wives also be subject in everything to their husbands. Husbands, love your wives, as Christ loved the church and gave himself up for her, that he might sanctify her, having cleansed her by the washing of water with the word, that he might present the church to himself in splendor, without spot or wrinkle or any such thing, that she might be holy and without blemish. Even so husbands should love their wives as their own bodies. He who loves his wife loves himself. For no man ever hates his own flesh, but nourishes and cherishes it, as Christ does the church, because we are members of his body. "For this reason a man shall leave his father and mother and be joined to his wife, and the two shall become one flesh." This mystery is a profound one, and I am saying that it refers to Christ and the church; however, let each one of you love his wife as himself, and let the wife see that she respects her husband. *Ephesians 5:21-33*

Father, thank you for my husband.
Give me the capacity to love him faithfully
   and consistently every day of my life.
Give me wisdom and confidence to express my
   love for him in ways that are obvious to him.
I need your grace to enable me to honor
   and respect him.
Let our love be an example to those
   around us, especially our children.
Make me a source of support and encouragement
   to him, especially when he is undergoing difficulties.
Amen. *Anonymous*

O Father, my heart is filled with a happiness so wonderful that I am almost afraid. This is my wedding day, and I pray thee that the beautiful joy of this morning may never grow dim with years of regret for the step I am about to take. Rather, may its memories become more sweet and tender with each passing anniversary.

Thou hast sent to me one who seems all worthy of my deepest regard. May I have the power to keep him ever true and loving as now and to prove indeed a helpmate, a sweetheart, a friend, a steadfast guiding star among all the temptations that beset the impulsive hearts of men. I pray that I may have skill to make home the best-loved place of all and to make its lights shine farther than any glow that would dim its radiance.

With thee I shall be able to meet the little mis-understandings and aches of my new life bravely. I know thou art with me as I start on my mission of womanhood, and will stay my path from failure all the way. May we walk with thee even to the end of our journey.

O Father, may our wedding day be blessed, and our marriage night hallowed. Sanctify my motherhood, if thou seest fit to grant me that privilege, and when all my youthful charms are faded, and the cares and lessons of life have left their touches, let physical fascination give way to the greater charm of com-panionship. And so may we walk hand-in-hand, down the highway of the Valley of Final Shadow, which we shall then be able to lighten with the sunshine of good and happy lives.

Our Father, this is my prayer. Amen.   *Anonymous*

My God, I thank you for the husband
   you gave me.
I feel as if we were born for each other.
The happiness I feel
   also comes with the obligation
   to love him as he loves me.
With tenderness I keep the memory
   of our early encounters.
I recall our efforts to fit together
   and to understand each other.
Sometimes it seems to me, my God,

that he is like the plant root
and I am the plant.
He is never separated from my being
and with time he more and more sustains my life
and enriches it.
My God, take good care of him
because I love him so much;
I love him just as he is.
Faithful to him, I want to be worthy of his love
and fulfill our common destiny
to the very end.
I hope that with your grace, my God,
I will live happily with him,
side by side,
fulfilling my role with all my heart.
Pour your blessing, my God,
over my husband's life,
over his work and concerns,
and make our lives become even more beautifully
united.
Amen.   *Hugo Schlesinger*
        Humberto Porto

Lord, we are sorry and we ask your forgiveness
that sometimes we show lack of respect, and
understanding and love;
that we neglect each other by neglecting to pray
for each other;
that we have often spoiled the perfect relationship

you planned for us;
and yet we also want to thank you
for the happiness we have known together
for the sadness we have faced together
for the problems we are overcoming together
for the love which you give us which is completely
unspoiled.
In the name of Jesus Christ, our Lord. *Christopher Idle*

Lord, draw near to my husband today. Let his mind turn often to you and his heart be set on your will. Strengthen him to do his work well and prosper all he undertakes. Help him where he is weak and teach him how to rely on you in everything. Give him wisdom for our family and show him how to lead us. Teach me to respect and support him. And use me, Lord, to make him the man you want him to be. Increase our love and protect our marriage from the evil one and worldly influence. In your mercy, Lord, establish my husband in your truth and your ways. *Anonymous*

Take scrupulous care never to irritate your husband, your household, or your parents by overmuch church-going, exaggerated seclusion, or neglect of your family duties. Don't let it make you censorious of others' conduct, or turn up your nose at conversations which fail to conform to your own lofty standards, for in all such matters charity must rule and enlighten us, so that we comply graciously with our neighbor's wishes in anything that is not contrary to God's law.

St. Francis de Sales

It is a happy thing when two souls meet who love each other only in order to love God better. *St. Francis de Sales*

Lord, help me love my husband and be patient with him especially since he does not know or acknowledge you. Help me to show him the care and mercy of Jesus in all my words and actions. Sometimes I feel so alone, frustrated, angry, and even bitter that he has not responded to you. O God, give me hope! Give me endurance to wait for you to work. And give me your heart for my husband, that I may see him as you see him, that I may love him as you love him. Hear my prayers for him, Lord. I entrust him to you. *Anonymous*

SIX

Living Single and Loving God

Preserve me, O God, for in thee I take refuge.
   I say to the LORD, "Thou art my Lord;
   I have no good apart from thee." . . .
The LORD is my chosen portion and my cup;
   thou holdest my lot.
The lines have fallen for me in pleasant places;
   yea, I have a goodly heritage.   *Psalm 16:1-2, 5-6*

Hear, O daughter, consider, and incline your ear;
   forget your people and your father's house;
   and the king will desire your beauty.
Since he is your lord, bow to him;
   the people of Tyre will sue your favor with gifts,
   the richest of the people with all kinds of wealth.
The princess is decked in her chamber with gold-
woven robes;
   in many colored robes she is led to the king,
   with her virgin companions, her escort, in her train.

With joy and gladness they are led along
  as they enter the palace of the king. *Psalm 45:10-15*

Lord, I trust you with my future. Whether you give me
a husband or whether you call me to be content
unmarried, let me be intimately aware of your lovingkindness toward me. Show me your provision as I wait
for your will to be fulfilled in my life. Give me
opportunities to serve those around me and the grace
to love others with your love. Most of all, Lord, let me
love you above all else, above all personal gain and
above all other loves. Amen. *Anonymous*

May nothing be dearer to me than You,
may nothing concern me more than You,
may nothing but Your sufferings cause me to mourn,
may nothing but You elate my heart,
may nothing make me sad but Your sufferings for my
    sins.
You alone are the One upon whom are centred my
    thoughts,
feelings, wishes and desires
Jesus, Jesus, Jesus—only You! *Basilea Schlink*

O my God! Blessed Trinity, I desire to love You and
make You loved, to work for the glorification of Holy
Church by saving souls on earth and delivering souls
suffering in Purgatory. I desire to accomplish Your will

perfectly and attain the degree of glory You have prepared for me in Your Kingdom. In a word I desire to be a saint, but I feel my powerlessness, and I ask You, O my God, to be Yourself my Sanctity.

Since You have so loved me as to give Your only Son to be my Saviour and my Spouse, the infinite treasures of His merits are mine, I offer them to You with joy, begging You to look at me only with the Face of Jesus between, and in His heart burning with Love.

St. Thérèse of Lisieux

O kind and merciful Savior, from my heart I earnestly desire to return Your love for love. My greatest sorrow is that You are not loved by people, and, in particular, that my own heart is so cold, so selfish, so ungrateful.

Keenly aware of my own weakness and poverty, I trust that Your own grace will enable me to offer You an act of pure love. And I wish to offer You this act of love in reparation for the coldness and neglect that are shown to You in the sacrament of Your love by Your creatures.

O Jesus, my supreme good, I love You, not for the sake of the reward which You have promised to those who love You, but purely for Yourself. I love You above all things that can be loved, above all pleasures, and above myself and all that is not You, promising in the presence of heaven and earth that I will live and die purely and simply in Your holy love, and that if to love You thus I must endure persecution and suffering, I am

completely satisfied and I will ever say with St. Paul:
Nothing will be able to separate us from the love of
God.

O Jesus, supreme master of all hearts, I love You, I
adore You, I praise You, I thank You, because I am now
all Yours. Rule over me and transform my soul into the
likeness of Yourself, so that it may bless and glorify You
forever in the abode of the saints. Amen.

Mary Margaret Alacoque

To me—
Jesus is my God.
Jesus is my spouse.
Jesus is my life.
Jesus is my only love.
Jesus is my all in all.
Jesus is my everything.
Jesus, I love with my whole heart, with my whole being.
I have given him all, even my sins, and he has espoused
me to himself in all tenderness and love.
Now and for life I am the spouse of my crucified
Spouse.
Amen.   *Mother Teresa of Calcutta*

Happy the enamored heart,
Thought centered on God alone,
Renouncing every creature for Him,
Finding in Him glory and contentment.
Living forgetful of self,

In God is all its intention,
Happy and so joyfully it journeys
Through waves of this stormy sea.   *St. Teresa of Avila*

Sweetest Jesus, Spouse Divine,
Whose is greater worthy than Thine
To be loved and honored.
Thou my Sun, whose radiant beams
Through my heart in glory stream
From Thy love so holy.
Joy Thou bringest to my heart,
Balm in suffering dost impart,
Thou art ever loving.
Who could ever happier be
Than the bride beloved by Thee,
To Thy love responding?
She rejoices, thrills and glows,
Sings for joy because she knows
She is so beloved.   *Basilea Schlink*

He (she) who desires nothing but God is rich and happy.   *St. Alphonsus de Liguori*

There is nothing so blessed as a devout religious, nothing so miserable as a religious without devotion.

St. Francis de Sales

SEVEN

Making Christ the Center of Your Home

Blessed is every one who fears the LORD,
　who walk in his ways!
You shall eat the fruit of the labor of your hands;
　you shall be happy, and it shall be well with you.
Your wife will be like a fruitful vine
　within your house;
your children will be like olive shoots
　around your table.
Lo, thus shall the man be blessed
　who fears the LORD.
The LORD bless you from Zion!
　May you see the prosperity of Jerusalem
　all the days of your life!
May you see your children's children!
　Peace be upon Israel!　*Psalm 128*

". . . but as for me and my house, we will serve the LORD." *Joshua 24:15b*

And let the peace of Christ rule in your hearts, to which indeed you were called in the one body. And be thankful. Let the word of Christ dwell in you richly, teach and admonish one another in all wisdom, and sing psalms and hymns and spiritual songs with thankfulness in your hearts to God. And whatever you do, in word or deed, do everything in the name of the Lord Jesus, giving thanks to God the Father through him. *Colossians 3:15-17*

O dear Jesus,
I humbly implore You to grant Your special graces to our family. May our home be the shrine of peace, purity, love, labor and faith. I beg You, dear Jesus, to protect and bless all of us, absent and present, living and dead.

O Mary,
loving Mother of Jesus, and our Mother, pray to Jesus for our family, for all the families of the world, to guard the cradle of the newborn, the schools of the young and their vocations.

Blessed Saint Joseph,
holy guardian of Jesus and Mary, assist us by your prayers in all the necessities of life. Ask of Jesus that special grace which He granted to you, to watch over

our home at the pillow of the sick and the dying, so that with Mary and with you, heaven may find our family unbroken in the Sacred Heart of Jesus. Amen.

Anonymous

For the family
Father, we pray for the family of all mankind that they may acknowledge you as their creator and provider; for the family of our nation that we may live in peace and encourage other nations to do likewise; for the families of this neighbourhood with whom you have chosen us to share your presence. Finally, for our own family that your peace may descend upon us so that from our inner awareness of your presence we may witness your love for the whole human family. *Michael Buckley*

The Christian home is not merely a community of human life. The precious gift of human life must be incorporated into and enriched by the very life of Christ. The family is rightly committed to preserve human values, but it must also focus on cultivating Christian values.

The members of the family can be tempted to think that only priests and religious have been entrusted with responsibility for the church. But this is far from being true. It is precisely at home that the children learn for the first time what it means to be "sharers of the promise . . . in Christ Jesus . . . through the preaching of the gospel" (Eph 3:6). As the Second Vatican Council teaches: "Christian spouses are cooperators with grace and witnesses of faith to each other, to their children, and to other members of the family. They are for their children the first heralds of faith and Christian education; they form them in the Christian life by their word and by their example. They help them use prudence in choosing their vocation. They favor greatly priestly and religious vocations if their children are so called" (AA, 11).

The Christian family is the first place where vocations are developed. It is a seminary or a novitiate for the children. Let us get rid of the false idea that Christianity is practiced only in church. Whatever takes place in the liturgy must be transferred to daily life. It must be lived at home. Then the home will become the place in which life in Christ grows and matures. Such a home is a true expression of the church. *Pope John Paul II*

Thank you, Father, for having created us and given us to each other in the human family.
Thank you for being with us in all our joys and sorrows, for your comfort in our sadness, your companionship in our loneliness.
Thank you for yesterday, today, tomorrow and for the whole of our lives.
Thank you for friends, for health and for grace.
May we live this and every day conscious of all that has been given to us. *Michael Buckley*

O Lord, it is wonderful to know that in your hands are the issues of life and death;
I don't want to take for granted any of your good gifts—even the breath I breathe;
I don't want to enjoy the strength of my limbs or the quickness of my mind—without thanks;
I don't want to become casual about the pleasant things about me—home and skies and flowers;
I don't want to live without concern for others—family and neighbours and friends.
I would not set about any part of this day—choosing what I will do, and refuse to do—without offering praise that I have so many interests and that you have given me power to choose.
Let no sense of well-being lead me into a foolish dependence on my own wisdom, my own strength. Without your love and strong keeping, I have no security. Keep me, O Lord. Amen.   *Rita Snowden*

Almighty God, You have called us to the holy state of Matrimony and have shared with us Your gift of creation. We thank You for making our love fruitful. May we be worthy representatives of You dear Lord in forming our children in Your knowledge and love. You have given us children, Almighty God, to teach in Your ways which will lead to their eternal home of heaven. May our children ever walk in the ways of your commandments and live according to the teachings of your holy Catholic Church. May our example dear

God, be such as to inspire our children to grow into the likeness of your Son, Jesus Christ. May we be firm but kind in discipline. May we stand as one united in authority so as to be consistent. May we never confuse permissiveness with love. May we teach our children respect for Your authority in ourselves and in all Your representatives upon earth.

May our home be as a Church, for You, Lord Jesus Christ, are present wherever two or three are gathered together in Your Name. May praises of God frequently rise from the lips and hearts of our family and may we all one day be united in our eternal home. Amen.

Anonymous

You will never be happy if your happiness depends on getting solely what you want. Change the focus. Get a new center. Will what God wills, and your joy no man shall take from you. . . . *Fulton Sheen*

For parents
Heavenly Father, from whom all parenthood comes, teach us so to understand our children that they may grow in your wisdom and love according to your holy will. Fill us with sensitive respect for the great gift of human life which you have committed to our care, help us to listen with patience to their worries and problems and give us the tolerance to allow them to develop, as individuals, as your Son did under the loving guidance of Mary and Joseph. *Michael Buckley*

The Importance of Family Prayer:

It honors God the Father from whom all families come.

It establishes a God-centered home life where God is praised, his word heard, and true fellowship experienced.

It enriches and sweetens family relationships.

It sets the right tone for each day and gives perspective for all family activities.

It helps to resolve conflicts, friction, and difficult relationships.

It strengthens family members to face the adversities of everyday life.

It gives opportunities for needs to be rightly expressed and therefore call family members on for support and love.

It transforms the home into a "little church" where God is worshiped, his word heard, his works proclaimed, his presence enjoyed, and his person loved.   *Anonymous*

EIGHT

Relationships at Work

Behold, how good and pleasant it is
  when brothers dwell in unity!
It is like the precious oil upon the head,
  running down upon the beard, upon the beard of
    Aaron,
  running down on the collar of his robes!
It is like the dew of Hermon,
  which falls on the mountains of Zion!
For there the LORD has commanded the blessing,
  life for ever more.   *Psalm 133*

He that takes vengeance will suffer vengeance from the
    Lord,
  and he will firmly establish his sins.
Forgive your neighbor the wrong he has done,
  and then your sins will be pardoned when you pray.
Does a man harbor anger against another,
  and yet seek for healing from the Lord?

Does he have no mercy toward a man like himself,
   and yet pray for his own sins?
If he himself, being flesh, maintains wrath,
   who will make expiation for his sins?
Remember the end of your life, and cease from enmity,
   remember destruction and death, and be true to the
     commandments.
Remember the commandments, and do not be angry
   with your neighbor:
  remember the covenant of the Most High, and
   overlook ignorance.   *Sirach 28:1-7*

Slaves, obey those who are in everything your human
masters, not with eye service, as men-pleasers, but in
singleness of heart, fearing the Lord. Whatever your
task, work heartily, as serving the Lord and not men,
knowing that from the Lord you will receive the
inheritance as your reward; you are serving the Lord
Christ. For the wrongdoer will be paid back for the
wrong he has done, and there is no partiality. Masters,
treat your slaves justly and fairly, knowing that you
also have a Master in heaven.   *Colossians 3:22-4:1*

Keep us, O God, from all pettiness.
Let us be large in thought, in word, in deed.
Let us be done with fault-finding and leave off all
   self-seeking.
May we put away all pretense and meet each other face

to face, without self pity and without prejudice.

May we never be hasty in judgment, and always be generous.

Let us always take time for all things, and make us to grow calm, serene and gentle.

Teach us to put into action our better impulses, to be straightforward and unafraid.

Grant that we may realize that it is the little things of life that create differences, that in the big things of life, we are as one.

And, O Lord God, let us not forget to be kind! Amen.

Mary Stewart

May I be no man's enemy, and may I be the friend of that which is eternal and abides.

May I never quarrel with those nearest me; and if I do, may I be reconciled quickly.

May I love, seek, and attain only that which is good.

May I wish for all men's happiness and envy none.

May I never rejoice in the ill-fortune of one who has wronged me.

May I win no victory that harms either me or my opponent.

May I reconcile friends who are angry with one another.

May I, to the extent of my power, give all needful help to my friends and all who are in want.

May I never fail a friend who is in danger.

May I respect myself. *Eusebius of Caesarea*

Father,
forgive me the petty sins
of a working day.
Forgive the curt remarks,
the mean self-interest
that misses opportunities
for caring, sharing, loving.

Lord,
as you do not bear grudges
against me, let me not bear grudges
against anyone.
As you do not cling
to the memory of my sins,
let me forget
the wrongs I have suffered.

Father,
forgive us our trespasses
as we forgive those
who trespass against us.   *Frank Topping*

Respect and concern for others
Grant me, O Lord, an understanding heart, that I may
see into the hearts of your people, and know their
strengths and weaknesses, their hopes and their des-
pairs, their efforts and failures, their need of love and
their need to love. Through my touch with them grant
comfort and hope, and the assurance that new life
begins at any age and on any day, redeeming the past,

sanctifying the present, and brightening the future with the assurance of your unfailing love, brought to me in Jesus Christ, your Son my Lord.   *George Appleton*

O God, our Father, help us all through this day so to live that we may bring help to others, credit to ourselves and to the name we bear, and joy to those that love us, and to you.
 Cheerful when things go wrong;
 Persevering when things are difficult;
 Serene when things are irritating.
Enable us to be;
 Helpful to those in difficulties;
 Kind to those in need;
 Sympathetic to those whose hearts are sore and sad.
Grant that;
 Nothing may make us lose our tempers;
 Nothing may take away our joy;
 Nothing may ruffle our peace;
 Nothing may make us bitter towards anyone.
So grant that through all this day all with whom we work, and all those whom we meet, may see in us the reflection of the master, whose we are, and whom we seek to serve. This we ask for your love's sake.
        William Barclay

Lord, I hurt someone today.
It's so easy to do.
Sometimes I hurt people accidentally,

when I talk without thinking.
Maybe we start out teasing or fooling around,
but it ends up with someone getting hurt.
Other times I know exactly what I'm doing.
I set out deliberately to hurt someone,
to get even with them.
And sometimes it gives me a feeling of power
to know I can make someone feel bad.
Was the hurt I gave today
accidental or deliberate?
I'm not even sure.
But I am sorry.
Forgive me, Lord.
I know there's enough pain in the world
without my adding to it.
Help me to apologize to the person I hurt.
Show me how I can make up for the pain I caused.
Make me more sensitive to the feelings of others.

                                            Ron and Lyn Klug

Let Martha be active without criticizing Mary, and
Mary contemplate without despising Martha, for the
Lord will always take the part of the one who is
censured.   *St. Francis de Sales*

There are only two duties that our Lord requires of us:
the love of God, and the love of our neighbour. And, in
my opinion, the surest sign for our discovering our love

to God is discovering our love to our neighbour. Be assured that the further you advance in the love of your neighbour, the more you are advancing in the love of God.

But alas, many worms lie gnawing at the roots of our love to our neighbour! Self-love, self-esteem, fault-finding, envy, anger, impatience, and scorn.

My sisters, our Lord expects works. Therefore when you see anyone sick, have compassion upon her as if she were yourself. Pity her. Fast that she may eat. Wake that she may sleep.

Again, when you hear anyone commended in praise, rejoice in it as much as if you were commended and praised yourself. This indeed should be easier because where true humility is, praise is prompted. Cover also your sister's defects as you would cover and not expose your own defects and faults.

As often as an occasion offers, lift up your neighbour's burden. Take it from her heart and put it upon yourself.   *St. Teresa of Avila*

In the home it is kindness;
In the business it is honesty;
In society it is courtesy;
In work it is fairness;
Toward the unfortunate it is sympathy;
Toward the weak it is help;
Toward the wicked it is resistance;

Toward the strong it is trust;
Toward the penitent it is forgiveness;
Toward the successful it is congratulation;
And toward God it is reverence and obedience.

Anonymous

NINE

Praying for Your Relatives and Friends

Pray for the peace of Jerusalem!
  "May they prosper who love you!
Peace be within your walls,
  and security within your towers!"
For my brethren and companions' sake
  I will say, "Peace be within you!"
For the sake of the house of the LORD, our God,
  I will seek your good.   *Psalm 122:6-9*

For this reason I bow my knees before the Father, from whom every family in heaven and on earth is named, that according to the riches of his glory he may grant you to be strengthened with might through his Spirit in the inner man, and that Christ may dwell in your hearts through faith; that you, being rooted and grounded in love, may have power to comprehend with all the saints what is the breadth and length and height and depth, and to know the love of Christ which surpasses

knowledge, that you may be filled with all the fulness
of God.   *Ephesians 3:14-19*

Listen to me your father, O children;
  and act accordingly, that you may be kept in safety.
For the Lord honored the father above the children,
  and he confirmed the right of the mother over her
    sons.
Whoever honors his father atones for sins,
  and whoever glorifies his mother is like one who lays
    up treasure.
Whoever honors his father will be gladdened by his
    own children,
  and when he prays he will be heard.
Whoever glorifies his father will have long life;
  and whoever obeys the Lord will refresh his mother;
  he will serve his parents as his masters.
Honor your father by word and deed,
  that a blessing from him may come upon you.
                                        Sirach 3:1-8

Lord Jesus Christ,
I praise and thank you for my parents and my brothers
    and sisters,
whom you have given me to cherish.
Surround them with your tender, loving care,
teach them to love and serve one another
in true affection,
and to look to you in all their needs.

I place them all in your care,
knowing that your love for them is greater
than my own.
Keep us close to one another in this life
and conduct us at the last to our true
and heavenly home.
Blessed be God for ever. Amen.   *Michael Buckley*

Loving Father, forgive me for my pride. I admit that I
need the wisdom of other more experienced mothers.
Give me the grace to overcome an independent spirit
and give me a teachable heart. Lead me to women that I
can learn from and use me to be a positive influence in
the lives of other mothers. Amen.   *Anonymous*

Almighty God, we entrust all who are dear to us to Thy
never-failing care and love, for this life and the life to
come; knowing that Thou art doing for them better
things than we can desire or pray for.

Book of Common Prayer

I pray thee, good Lord Jesus, by the love thou hadst for
thy young disciple John, to make me thankful for all
thou hast given me in my friend. Bless him exceedingly
above all that I can ask or think. Help us to be one in
heart through all separations, and walk together in the
path of thy service, and finally unite us in the place
where love is perfect and immortal, even with thyself.

William Bright

O God, our heavenly Father, who has commanded us to love one another as thy children, and has ordained the highest friendship in the bond of thy Spirit, we beseech thee to maintain and preserve us always in the same bond, to thy glory, and our mutual comfort, with all those to whom we are bound by any special tie, either of nature or of choice; that we may be perfected together in that love which is from above, and which never faileth when all other things shall fail.

Send down the dew of thy heavenly grace upon us, that we may have joy in each other that passeth not away; and having lived together in love here, according to thy commandment, may live for ever together with thee, being made one in thee, in thy glorious kingdom hereafter, through Jesus Christ our Lord.   *George Hickes*

Be pleased, O Lord, to remember my friends, all that have prayed for me, and all that have done me good.

Do good to them and return all their kindness a double time, rewarding them with blessings and sanctifying them with Thy graces.

Let all my family and kindred, my neighbours and acquaintances receive the benefit of my prayers, and the blessing of God; the comforts and supports of Thy providence, and the sanctification of Thy Spirit.

Jeremy Taylor

Let your friendship be grave, simple and edifying in all things. Love God, his work, your community, and your salvation, still more than the person in question.

Francois Fénélon

TEN

Hospitality

Stretch forth your hand to the poor,
  so that your blessing may be complete.
Give graciously to all the living,
  and withhold not kindness from the dead.
Do not fail those who weep,
  but mourn with those who mourn.
Do not shrink from visiting a sick man,
  because for such deeds you will be loved.
In all you do, remember the end of your life,
  and then you will never sin.   *Sirach 7:32-36*

The point is this: he who sows sparingly will also reap sparingly, and he who sows bountifully will also reap bountifully. Each one must do as he has made up his mind, not reluctantly or under compulsion, for God loves a cheerful giver. And God is able to provide you with every blessing in abundance, so that you may always have enough of everything and may provide in abundance for every good work. As it is written,
  "He scatters abroad, he gives to the poor;

his righteousness endures for ever.''

He who supplies seed to the sower and bread for food will supply and multiply your resources and increase the harvest of your righteousness.

You will be enriched in every way for great generosity, which through us will produce thanksgiving to God; for the rendering of this service not only supplies the wants of the saints but also overflows in many thanksgivings to God. Under the test of this service, you will glorify God by your obedience in acknowledging the gospel of Christ, and by the generosity of your contribution for them and for all others; while they long for you and pray for you, because of the surpassing grace of God in you. Thanks be to God for his inexpressible gift!   *2 Corinthians 9:6-15*

And let us not grow weary in well-doing, for in due season we shall reap, if we do not lose heart. So then, as we have opportunity, let us do good to all men, and especially to those who are of the household of faith.

Galatians 6:9-10

Do not neglect to show hospitality to strangers, for thereby some have entertained angels unawares.

Hebrews 13:2

God, make the door of this house wide enough to receive all who need human love and fellowship, narrow enough to shut out all envy, pride and strife.

Make its threshold smooth enough to be no stumbling-block to children, nor to straying feet, but rugged and strong enough to turn back the tempter's power. God, make the door of this house the gateway to Thine eternal kingdom.   *On the door of St. Stephen's in London*

In your great mercy, O Lord, grant that this may be a good day in this home.
   Save us from becoming casual with each other;
   Save us from lack of self-discipline;
   Save us from discourtesy.
Bless any who shall come over our doorstep; any who shall sit at our table; or share talk with us over the 'phone.
Let us use our home, and the treasured things we have gathered about us to give others joy.
Make us each discreet in our conversation, and loving and loyal to each other.
And to you we would give all the glory and praise. Amen.   *Rita Snowden*

O God, the refuge of the poor, the strength of those who toil, and the Comforter of all who sorrow, we commend to your mercy the unfortunate and needy in whatever land they may be. You alone know the number and extent of their sufferings and trials. Look down, Father of mercies, at those unhappy families suffering from war and slaughter, from hunger and disease, and other severe trials. Spare them, O Lord, for it is truly a time for mercy.   *St. Peter Canisius*

Dearest Lord, may I see you today and every day in the person of your sick, and, whilst nursing them, minister unto you.

Though you hide yourself behind the unattractive disguise of the irritable, the exacting, the unreasonable, may I still recognize you, and say: "Jesus, my patient, how sweet it is to serve you."

Lord, give me this seeing faith, then my work will never be monotonous, I will ever find joy in humouring the fancies and gratifying the wishes of all poor sufferers.

O beloved sick, how doubly dear you are to me, when you personify Christ; and what a privilege is mine to be allowed to tend you.

Sweetest Lord, make me appreciative of the dignity of my high vocation, and its many responsibilities. Never permit me to disgrace it by giving way to coldness, unkindness, or impatience.

And O God, while you are Jesus my patient, deign also to be to me a patient Jesus, bearing with my faults, looking only to my intention, which is to love and serve you in the person of each one of your sick.

Lord, increase my faith, bless my efforts and work, now and for evermore. Amen.   *Mother Teresa of Calcutta*

God of love, whose compassion never fails; we bring to you the sufferings of all mankind; the needs of the homeless; the cry of prisoners; the pains of the sick and injured; the sorrow of the bereaved; the helplessness of the aged and weak. Strengthen and relieve them, Father, according to their various needs and your great mercy; for the sake of your Son our Saviour Jesus Christ. *St. Anselm*

ELEVEN

Your Health

Be gracious to me, O LORD, for I am in distress;
   my eye is wasted from grief, my soul and my body
     also.
For my life is spent with sorrow
   and my years with sighing;
my strength fails because of my misery,
   and my bones waste away. . . .
Let thy face shine on thy servant;
   save me in thy steadfast love!   *Psalm 31:9-10, 16*

I said, In the noontide of my days I must depart;
I am consigned to the gates of Sheol
   for the rest of my years.
I said, I shall not see the LORD
   in the land of the living;
I shall look upon man no more
   among the inhabitants of the world.
My dwelling is plucked up and removed from me
   like a shepherd's tent;
like a weaver I have rolled up my life;

he cuts me off from the loom;
from day to night thou dost bring me to an end;
   I cry for help until morning;
like a lion he breaks all my bones;
   from day to night thou dost bring me to an end.
Like a swallow or a crane I clamor,
   I moan like a dove.
My eyes are weary with looking upward.
   O Lord, I am oppressed; be thou my security!
But what can I say? For he has spoken to me,
   and he himself has done it.
All my sleep has fled
   because of the bitterness of my soul.
O Lord, by these things men live,
   and in all these is the life of my spirit.
   Oh, restore me to health and make me live!
Lo, it was for my welfare
   that I had great bitterness;
but thou hast held back my life
   from the pit of destruction,
for thou hast cast all my sins behind thy back.
For Sheol cannot thank thee,
   death cannot praise thee;
those who go down to the pit cannot hope
   for thy faithfulness.
The living, the living, he thanks thee,
   as I do this day;
The father makes known to the children
   thy faithfulness.

The LORD will save me,
  and we will sing to stringed instruments
all the days of our life,
  at the house of the Lord. *Isaiah 38:10-20*

Honor the physician with the honor due him,
    according to your need of him,
  for the Lord created him;
for healing comes from the Most High,
  and he will receive a gift from the king.
The skill of the physician lifts up his head,
  and in the presence of great men he is admired. . . .
My son, when you are sick do not be negligent,
  but pray to the Lord, and he will heal you.
Give up your faults and direct your hands aright,
  and cleanse your heart from all sin.
Offer a sweet-smelling sacrifice, and a memorial
    portion of fine flour,
  and pour oil on your offering, as much as you can
    afford.
And give the physician his place,
  for the Lord created him;
  let him not leave you, for there is need of him.
There is a time when success lies in the hands of
    physicians,
  for they too will pray to the Lord
that he should grant them success in diagnosis
  and in healing, for the sake of preserving life.

He who sins before his Maker,
>   may he fall into the care of a physician.
>   *Sirach 38:1-3, 9-15*

O God, your gift of health has made such a difference to
>   my day—
>   I have been able to rise and set about things;
>   I have been able to choose some activities and reject
>   some;
>   I have been able to sustain continuous effort.
I do not want to forget those who have been house-
bound today, those bed-fast, those sick, and frail;
I do not want to forget those approaching an operation—
especially whose who are fearful;
I do not want to forget those lying in the hospital, those
who have been there a long time.
I pray for all who tend those dependent on them
today—family, friends, neighbours;
I pray for doctors and surgeons and specialists, for
research workers, and all seeking new causes and
cures;
I pray for all who foster schemes of health and well-
being in the community.
Bless all little children, trustingly and safely tucked in;
All tired and weary workers, glad that night has come;
All sleepless people, and the old and frail, and those at
the point of death.
Bring us all to a new day—ready to begin again. In
Christ's name.   *Rita Snowden*

I am ill, Lord;
   come and heal me.
You can protect me and free me
   from all those evils of body and mind.
I have confidence in your miraculous power;
   I invoke your name
   so that you can assist me
   in my distress
   and speed my cure.
Believe me, Lord,
   I am learning
   the great lessons of humanness and patience,
   of gratitude and solidarity,
   which suffering brought me.
You, who are the source of all kindness
   and of all life,
   alleviate my pain.
Take away from me all shadow of depression,
   and strengthen my spirit,
   so that I can withstand everything
   without a word of despair or rebellion.
I am in your hands today as always.
Restore me, that I may return
   to my work,
   to surroundings of family and friends.
I need healing, Lord;
   come and heal me.
Amen.   *Humberto Porto*
          Hugo Schlesinger

Lord, let this sickness, like that of Lazarus, be unto the Father's glory and for the good of those who stand by. I must see to it that whatever I have to suffer is not wasted but is offered to the Father, and also that I do not give cause for disedification to those who have to wait on me. Inspire me during my illness at least to think of you occasionally: I do not want to make this time, so far as prayer is concerned, a blank. If my regular practices have to be abandoned, show me what new ones I may substitute. Give me, I pray you, a more vivid awareness of your presence, so as to make up for the kind of willed recollection which I try to maintain when I am well.   *Hubert van Zeller*

My strength fails; I feel only weakness, irritation and depression. I am tempted to complain and to despair. What has become of the courage I was so proud of, and that gave me so much self-confidence? In addition to my pain, I have to bear the shame of my fretful feebleness. Lord, destroy my pride; leave it no resource. How happy I shall be if you can teach me by these terrible trials, that I am nothing, that I can do nothing, and that you are all!   *Francois Fénélon*

Lord, bless all means that are used for my recovery, and restore me to my health in thy good time; but if otherwise thou hast appointed for me, thy blessed will be done. O draw me away from an affection for things below, and fill me with an ardent desire after heaven.

Lord, fit me for thyself, and then call me to those joys unspeakable and full of glory, when thou pleasest, and that for the sake of thy only Son, Jesus, my Saviour. Amen.   *Thomas Ken*

Grant, Lord, that as you sent this sickness to me, you will also send your Holy Spirit into my heart so that my present illness may be sanctified and used as a school in which I may learn to know the greatness of my misery and the riches of your mercy. May I be so humbled at my misery that I despair not of your mercy and thus renounce all confidence in myself and every other creature so that I may put the whole of my salvation in your all-sufficient merits.   *Lewis Bayley*

Lord, you gave me health and I forgot you. You take it away and I come back to you. What infinite compassion that God, in order to give himself to me, takes away his gifts which I allowed to come between me and him. Lord, take away everything that is not you. All is yours. You are the Lord. Dispose everything, comforts, success, health. Take all the things that possess me instead of you that I may be wholly yours.

Francois Fénélon

Lord, let us make sickness itself a prayer.
St. Francis de Sales

Part III

Lord, Comfort Me

ONE

For Times of Loneliness and Depression

I call upon thee, for thou wilt answer me, O God;
   incline thy ear to me, hear my words.
Wondrously show thy steadfast love,
   O savior of those who seek refuge
   from their adversaries at thy right hand.
Keep me as the apple of thy eye;
   hide me in the shadow of thy wings,
from the wicked who despoil me, my deadly enemies
    who surround me.   *Psalm 17:6-9*

But thou, O LORD, be not far off!
   O thou my help, hasten to my aid!
Deliver my soul from the sword,
   my life from the power of the dog!
Save me from the mouth of the lion,
   my afflicted soul from the horns of the wild oxen!
       Psalm 22:19-21

Do not give yourself over to sorrow,
  and do not afflict yourself deliberately.
Gladness of heart is the life of man,
  and the rejoicing of a man is length of days.
Distract your soul and comfort your heart,
  and remove sorrow far from you,
for sorrow has destroyed many,
  and there is no profit in it.
Jealousy and anger shorten life,
  and anxiety brings on old age too soon.
A man of cheerful and good heart
  will give heed to the food he eats.   *Sirach 30:21-24*

O my God, give me thy grace so that the things of this earth and things more naturally pleasing to me, may not be as close as thou art to me. Keep thou my eyes, my ears, my heart from clinging to the things of this world. Break my bonds, raise my heart. Keep my whole being fixed on thee. Let me never lose sight of thee; and while I gaze on thee, let my love of thee grow more and more every day.   *John Henry Cardinal Newman*

Show me how to approach my sense of being alone and cut off so that it may not be any longer a condition to be dreaded, but rather seen as a means to closer dependence upon you. Let my soul learn in solitude the lesson of your presence.   *A Book of Private Prayer*

My Lord and my God,
take me from all that keeps me from you.

My Lord and my God,
grant me all that leads me to you.
My Lord and my God,
take me from myself and give me completely to you.

St. Nicholas von Flue

Nights can be long and so lonely
   filled with such anguish and pain,
But joy cometh in the morning
   Like sunshine after the rain.
Sometimes your heart can be aching
   Filled with such grief and sorrow,
But joy cometh in the morning
   Bringing hope for the morrow.
For God hath not always promised
   Sunshine and blue skies above,
But joy cometh in the morning
   Bringing God's peace and His love.
They say it always seems darkest
   in the hours before the dawn,
But joy cometh in the morning
   Giving us faith to go on.
Thus we should trust Jesus always
   Give Him each sorrow and pain
For joy cometh in the morning
   Like sunshine after the rain.   *Mary E. Harrington*

Father, you do not protect us against catastrophes but
in them you come to our aid. It is in the very midst of
the tempest and misfortune that a wonderful zone of

peace, serenity and joy bursts in us if we dwell in your grace. You do not help us before we have helped ourselves, but when we are at the end of our resources you manifest yourself, and we begin to know that you have been there all the time.   *Louis Evely*

What avails melancholy forebodings, and indulgence of feelings which can never alter the event of things?

One should, rather, look at life's realities as they were—guided by a just and merciful Protector who orders every occurrence in its time and place.

Elizabeth Seton

Gloom is no Christian temper ... *John Henry Cardinal Newman*

TWO

For Blessing and Help

How precious is thy steadfast love, O God!
  The children of men take refuge in the shadow of thy
    wings.
They feast on the abundance of thy house,
  and thou givest them drink from the river of thy
    delights.
For with thee is the fountain of life,
  in thy light do we see light.
O continue thy steadfast love to those who know thee,
  and thy salvation to the upright of heart!

Psalm 36:7-10

The LORD answer you in the day of trouble!
  The name of the God of Jacob protect you!
May he send you help from the sanctuary.
  and give you support from Zion.
May he remember all your offerings
  and regard with favor your burnt sacrifices!
May he grant you your heart's desire,
  and fulfil all your plans!

May we shout for joy over your victory
    and in the name of our God set up our banners!
May the Lord fulfil all your petitions!   *Psalm 20:1-5*

Show signs anew, and work further wonders;
    make thy hand and thy right arm glorious. . . .
Bear witness to those whom thou didst create in the
        beginning,
    and fulfil the prophecies spoken in thy name.
Reward those who wait for thee,
    and let thy prophets be found trustworthy.
Harken, O Lord, to the prayer of thy servants,
    according to the blessing of Aaron for thy people,
and all who are on the earth will know
    that thou art the Lord, the God of the ages.
                                        Sirach 36:6, 15-17

Grant us, we beseech thee, O Lord, grace to follow thee
whithersoever thou goest. In little daily duties to which
thou callest us, bow down our wills to simple obedience, patience under pain or provocation, strict truth-
fulness of word or manner, humility and kindness. In
great acts of duty or perfection, if thou shouldst call us
to them, uplift us to sacrifice and heroic courage, that in
all things, both small and great, we may be imitators of
thy dear Son, even Jesus Christ our Lord.
                                        Christina Rossetti

Teach us to know you, our God, and enable us to do your will as we ought to do. Give us hearts full of love for you, full of trust, full of faithfulness. May no temptations rock us, no tribulations drive us from you. May all that befalls us draw us closer in love and trust and fit us for your heavenly kingdom. Amen.

Benjamin Jenks

May the road rise to meet you,
May the wind be always at your back,
May the sun shine warm on your face,
The rain fall softly on your fields;
and until we meet again,
May God hold you in the palm of his hand.

An Old Gaelic Blessing

He is my strength
in present lack;
The moving forward,
even when there seems
no progress.
He is my freedom
when self would imprison;
The victory that overcomes
the darkest hour.
He is the peace
with arms outstretched
to free the inner toil;

He is my shield
and advocate,
A shelter from
the storm.
Roxie Lusk Smith

The Lord bless us and keep us. The Spirit of the Lord cleanse and purify our inmost hearts, and enable us to shun all evil. The Lord enlighten our understandings and cause the Light of his Truth to shine into our hearts. The Lord fill us with faith and love towards him. The Lord be with us day and night, in our coming and going out, in our sorrow and in our joy, and bring us at length into his eternal rest. *Unknown*

Remember, O Lord, of what I am made, that I am but human. Take pity on my weakness, support my frail nature. Thou knowest the temptations I suffer, how they surge within me, and the storms they raise in me. Thou knowest well. *St. Isidore*

O God, animate us to cheerfulness. May we have a joyful sense of our blessings, learn to look on the bright circumstances of our lot, and maintain a perpetual contentedness. Preserve us from despondency and from yielding to dejection. Teach us that nothing can hurt us if, with true loyalty of affection, we keep Thy commandments and take refuge in Thee.

William E. Channing

When spirits are low
   and your faith seems to wane,
Ask our dear Lord
   to help and sustain.
When troubles pile up
   and you can't seem to cope,
Ask our dear Father
   to help you find hope.
When the blues take over
   and there isn't a cure,
Ask the Master,
   He'll help you endure.
When, in tears, you see
   your dreams go wrong,
Ask our Saviour
   to help you be strong.
When life's road seems too rocky
   and you struggle in vain,
Ask our Saviour to help,
   He, too, suffered pain.
Just kneel in prayer
   and your needs reveal . . .
The Father will hear,
   He'll ever comfort and heal.
Jesus has promised
   He'll help until the end . . .
Things must turn out right
   when we have such a Friend.   *Mabel Isley Catron*

THREE

For Times of Trouble

My God, my God, why hast thou forsaken me?
  Why are thou so far from helping me, from the words
    of my groaning?
O my God, I cry by day, but thou dost not answer;
  and by night, but find no rest.
Yet thou art holy,
  enthroned on the praises of Israel.
In thee our fathers trusted;
  they trusted, and thou didst deliver them.
To thee they cried, and were saved;
  in thee they trusted, and were not disappointed.
But I am a worm, and no man;
  scorned of men, and despised by the people.
All who see me mock at me,
  they make mouths at me, they wag their heads;
"He committed his cause to the LORD; let him deliver
      him,
  let him rescue him, for he delights in him!"
Yet thou art he who took me from the womb;
  thou didst keep me safe upon my mother's breasts.

Upon thee was I cast from my birth,
   and since my mother bore me thou hast been my
      God.
Be not far from me,
   for trouble is near
   and there is none to help.   *Psalm 22:1-12*

God is our refuge and strength,
   a very present help in trouble.
Therefore we will not fear though the earth should
      change,
   though the mountains shake in the heart of the sea;
though its waters roar and foam,
   though the mountains tremble with its tumult.
The LORD of hosts is with us;
   the God of Jacob is our refuge.   *Psalm 46:1-3, 7*

Consequently, he is able for all time to save those who
draw near to God through him, since he always lives to
make intercession for them.   *Hebrews 7:25*

Almighty God, the refuge of all that are distressed,
grant unto us that, in all trouble of this our mortal life,
we may flee to the knowledge of your lovingkindness
and tender mercy; that so, sheltering ourselves therein,
the storms of life may pass over us, and not shake the
peace of God that is within us. Whatsoever this life may
bring us, grant that it may never take from us the full
faith that you are our Father. Grant us your light, that

we may have life, through Jesus Christ our Lord—
Amen.   *George Dawson*

Lord Jesus,
You know what pain is like.
You know
the torture of the scourge upon your back,
the sting of the thorns upon your brow,
the agony of the nails in your hands.
You know what I'm going through just now.
Help me
to bear my pain
gallantly, cheerfully and patiently,
And help me to remember
that I will never be tried
above what I am able to bear,
and that you are with me,
even in this valley of the deep dark shadow.
In ev'ry pang that rends the heart,
The Man of Sorrows had a part;
He sympathises with our grief,
And to the suff'rer sends relief.   *William Barclay*

O God, by your mercy strengthen us who lie exposed
to the rough storms of troubles and temptations. Help
us against our own negligence and cowardice, and
defend us from the treachery of our unfaithful hearts.
Help us, we implore you, and bring us to your safe
haven of peace and happiness.   *St. Augustine of Hippo*

May the strength of God pilot us.
May the power of God preserve us.
May the wisdom of God instruct us.
May the hand of God protect us.
May the way of God direct us.
May the shield of God defend us.
May the host of God guard us against the snares
    of the Evil One and the temptations of the world.

St. Patrick

Cast all your cares on God! That anchor holds.

Alfred Lord Tennyson

No matter what your trials are
    Or how big your mountain seems;
The Lord is there to see you through,
    He'll go to all extremes.
So, if your cross seems hard to bear
    And you know not what to do;
The One who loves you most of all
    Will be there to see you through.
And when your life seems empty
    And skies look gray, not blue;
You'll feel the nearness of the One
    Who's there to see you through.
Oh, friend, I've known the heartache
    When my rainbow lost its hue!
But like all things, it's passing.
    He was there to see me through. *Helen Parker*

It doesn't matter, really,
    how great the pressure is;
It only matters where the pressure lies. See that it never
comes between you and the Lord—then, the greater
the pressure, the more it presses you to His breast.

Hudson Taylor

FOUR

For Peace and Refreshment

The LORD is my shepherd, I shall not want;
  he makes me lie down in green pastures.
He leads me beside still waters;
  he restores my soul.
He leads me in paths of righteousness
  for his name's sake.
Even though I walk through the valley of the shadow
    of death,
  I fear no evil;
  for thou art with me
  thy rod and thy staff,
  they comfort me.   *Psalm 23:1-4*

O LORD, my heart is not lifted up,
  my eyes are not raised too high;
I do not occupy myself with things
  too great and too marvelous for me.
But I have calmed and quieted my soul,

like a child quieted at its mother's breast;
like a child that is quieted is my soul.
O Israel, hope in the Lord,
from this time forth and for evermore.   *Psalm 131:1-3*

"Come to me, all who labor and are heavy laden, and I will give you rest. Take my yoke upon you, and learn from me; for I am gentle and lowly in heart, and you will find rest for your souls. For my yoke is easy, and my burden is light."   *Matthew 11:28-30*

Deep and silent and cool as a broad, still, tree-shaded
    river
Is the peace of thy presence, thou rest of our souls.
From the thousand problems of this our hurrying life
We turn, with silent joy, to plunge in thee,
To steep our souls in thy quiet depths
Where no clamour of earth disturbs our perfect
    content.
Thou art our home and refuge;
In thee we are safe and at peace:
Ever in the din and hurry of the world
We know that thou art near,
We know that close at hand—closer than our little
    life—
Floweth that silent river of thy presence and love.
In a moment we may be with thee and in thee,
In a moment be surrounded and soaked in thy peace:
In a moment, as this loud world clangs round us,

We may rest secure in the bliss of thine eternity.
John S. Hoyland

O Lord, whose way is perfect: Help us, we pray thee, always to trust in thy goodness; that walking with thee in faith, and following thee in all simplicity, we may possess quiet and contented minds, and cast all our care on thee, because thou carest for us; for the sake of Jesus Christ our Lord.　*Christina Rossetti*

O God, our Father, we thank you for this time of rest from our daily work and our daily business.
We thank you for time to spend with our family and in the circle of those most dear.
We thank you for the open road, and the hills and the seashore, and for the clean wind upon our faces.
We thank you for games to play, for new places to see, new people to meet, new things to do.
Grant that the days of our holiday may refresh us in body and in mind, so that we may come back to work the better, because we rested awhile: through Jesus Christ our Lord. Amen.　*William Barclay*

O God, our Father, we thank you for this your own day.
We thank you for this day's rest, in which we lay aside our daily work and tasks to relax our bodies, to refresh our minds, and to strengthen our spirits.
We thank you for this day's worship, in which we lay

aside our cares and our anxieties to concentrate our
every thought on you alone.
We thank you for your church. We thank you for the
fellowship we enjoy within it; for the teaching which is
given to us; for the guidance for life and living which we
receive.
We thank you for the reading of your word, for the
preaching of your truth, for the singing of your praise,
for the prayers of your people, and for the sacraments
of your grace.
Grant that in this day of yours we may receive such
strength and guidance, that we shall be enabled to go
out to walk with you, and not to fall from you, in all the
days of this week which lies ahead: through Jesus
Christ our Lord. Amen.   *William Barclay*

Eternal Father, I thank you for the days of rest
　　which I was permitted to enjoy;
　　they were truly healthy
　　for my body and for my mind.
How shall I express my gratitude
　　for this precious and fruitful opportunity?
Eternal Father, I praise you for the sky and the sun,
　　for the water and the trees, which express for me
　　the beauty of the world you created.
I praise you for the kind hearts I met,
　　who extended unending favors to me during my trip.
I praise you for the smiling faces
　　that relaxed me,

and left me reconciled
   with the joy of living.
I praise you and thank you, Eternal Father,
   because I returned home healthy and safe.
Now restored, I undertake my duties again,
   having known the pleasant and happy experiences
   I had during my vacation.
I thank you for everything,
   now and always.
Amen.   *Humberto Porto*
         Hugo Schlesinger

Blessed are you, Lord,
   for the relaxation of this day,
   which is consecrated to you.
I join all human beings
   who serve you with reverence and love,
   and glorify you by honest and good deeds.
Blessed are you, Lord,
   because today you let me restore
   my strength
   for the daily work
   that dignifies my life
   and extends your creative work.
Blessed are you, Lord,
   for the opportunity to have another day
   to spend with my family and friends;
   they are part of my life,
   and I entrust them to your care.

Blessed are you, Lord,
    for the well-being of this quiet day,
    which permits me to gratefully regain
    the enthusiasm and the joy of living.
Blessed are you, Lord,
    because you today restore my spirit
    so that I can always walk
    in your light
    and be accompanied by your caring presence.
Amen.   *Humberto Porto*
        Hugo Schlesinger

When peace, like a river, attendeth my way,
When sorrows like sea billows roll—
Whatever my lot, Thou hast taught me to say,
It is well, it is well with my soul.
It is well, it is well with my soul.
Though Satan should buffet,
Tho' trials should come,
Let this blest assurance control,
That Christ has regarded my helpless estate,
And hath shed His own blood for my soul.
My sin—oh, the bliss of this glorious tho't:
My sin not in part, but the whole
Is nail'd to the cross and I bear it no more,
Praise the Lord, praise the Lord, O my soul!
        Horatio G. Spafford
        Philip P. Bliss

Deep peace of the Running Wave to you.
Deep peace of the Flowing Air to you.
Deep peace of the Quiet Earth to you.
Deep peace of the Shining Stars to you.
Deep peace of the Son of Peace to you.

Celtic Benediction

FIVE

For Times of Insecurity and Inadequacy

Be gracious to me, O LORD, for I am in distress
    my eye is wasted from grief,
    my soul and my body also.
For my life is spent with sorrow
    and my years with sighing;
my strength fails because of my misery,
    and my bones waste away.
I am the scorn of my adversaries,
    a horror to my neighbors,
an object of dread to my acquaintances;
    those who see me in the street flee from me.
I have passed out of mind like one who is dead;
    I have become like a broken vessel. . . .
But I trust in thee, O LORD,
    I say, "Thou art my God."   *Psalm 31:9-12, 14*

For God alone my soul waits in silence,
　for my hope is from him.
He only is my rock and my salvation,
　my fortress; I shall not be shaken.
On God rests my deliverance and my honor;
　my mighty rock, my refuge is God.　*Psalm 62:5-7*

God, our Father, I turn to you in my unrest because I cannot see any way out of the present situation which troubles my spirit. In my confusion I turn to you for help and guidance because you alone can help me and nothing is impossible to you. Light up my life with faith, strengthen me in hope and fill me with love, so that I may rest in your providence which alone knows what is for my peace.　*Michael Buckley*

Give me, O Lord, a steadfast heart which no unworthy thought can drag downwards; an unconquered heart which no tribulation can wear out; an upright heart which no unworthy purpose may tempt aside. Bestow upon me also, O Lord my God, understanding to know thee, diligence to seek thee, wisdom to find thee, and a faithfulness that may finally embrace thee; through Jesus Christ, our Lord.　*St. Thomas Aquinas*

Give me thy grace, O Lord, that I may never envy any good man's or woman's love because they do either love God and his people more than I. Make me to rejoice in other men's gifts, and not envy them, because they be better than mine; but rather to give thanks for them with all my heart, desiring that they be increased in them and in me.   *Christian Prayer*

O Lord, stop me from feeling jealous. Help me to share in my friends' and enemies' successes, and not to be jealous when they are praised and thanked and I am not. Live in me, O Lord, and work through me, and let me see my successes as yours that I may be one with you as you are with the Father.

Help me too not to be jealous when those I love seem to love others more than me, but make me love you more and to find you increasingly in all men.   *Etta Gullick*

Let nothing disturb you,
Nothing affright you.
All things are passing,
God never changes.
Patience obtains all:
Whoever has God
Lacks nothing else.
God alone suffices.   *St. Theresa of Avila*

Coward and wayward and weak,
I change with the changing sky.
Today so eager and brave,
Tomorrow not willing to try.
But He never gives in,

And we two will win,
Jesus and I.   *Corrie ten Boom*

When you fail to measure up to your Christian privilege, be not discouraged for discouragement is a form
of pride. The reason you are sad is because you looked
to yourself and not to God; to your failing not to His
love. You will shake off your faults more readily when
you love God than when you criticize yourselves. The
sick person looks happily at the physician, not at his
wounds.   *Fulton Sheen*

SIX

For Freedom from Sin

For I am ready to fall
  and pain is ever with me.
I confess my iniquity,
  I am sorry for my sin.
Those who are my foes without cause are mighty
  and many are those who hate me wrongfully.
Those who render me evil for good
  are my adversaries because I follow after good.
Do not forsake me, O LORD!
  O my God, be not far from me!
Make haste to help me,
  O Lord, my salvation!   *Psalm 38:17-22*

"And now, Lord, for what do I wait?
  My hope is in thee.
Deliver me from all my transgressions.
  Make me not the scorn of the fool!"   *Psalm 39:7-8*

Have mercy on me, O God, according to thy steadfast
    love;

according to thy abundant mercy blot out my
　　transgressions.
Wash me thoroughly from my iniquity,
　　and cleanse me from my sin!
For I know my transgressions,
　　and my sin is ever before me.
Against thee, thee only, have I sinned,
　　and done that which is evil in thy sight,
so that thou art justified in thy sentence
　　and blameless in thy judgment.
Behold, I was brought forth in iniquity,
　　and in sin did my mother conceive me.
Behold, thou desirest truth in the inward being;
　　therefore teach me wisdom in thy secret heart.
Purge me with hyssop, and I shall be clean;
　　wash me, and I shall be whiter than snow.
Fill me with joy and gladness;
　　let the bones which thou hast broken rejoice.
Hide thy face from my sins,
　　and blot out all my iniquities.
Create in me a clean heart, O God,
　　and put a new and right spirit within me.
Cast me not away from thy presence,
　　and take not thy Holy Spirit from me.
Restore to me the joy of thy salvation,
　　and uphold me with a willing spirit.　　*Psalm 51:1-12*

Oh, God, touch my heart today
And cleanse me from all sin,

Put your love and joy inside
And keep it safe within
Till someone comes along
And needs my help
To lift their loads today,
Then may I reach inside my heart
and give love and joy away.   *Mildred H. Bell*

I humbly beg of thee, O merciful Father, that this present affliction may strengthen my faith, which thou sawest was growing weak; fix my hope which was staggering, quicken my devotion which was languishing, reunite me to my first love which I was forsaking, rekindle my charity which was cooling, revive my zeal which was dying, confirm my obedience which was wavering, recover my patience which was fainting, mortify my pride which was presuming; and perfect my repentance which was daily decaying: for all these and the like infirmities to which my soul is exposed, O make thy affliction my care. Amen.   *Thomas Ken*

Lord Trinity, Faithful God, I desire to be ever faithful to Your Commandments but most of all to Your plan in my life. I want to live in the present moment, benefitting by the past and looking forward to the future with confidence. Make me a faithful friend to my neighbor so I will have the love to endure their weaknesses and the courage to stand by them when they are in need. You were so loyal, Lord Jesus, to all

Your Apostles even though they were not faithful to You. You are the same with me—You are always faithful no matter how ungrateful I am. You give me grace to be repentant after I sin and You give me merit when I manage to accomplish some unselfish deed. You are always there when I need You and You wait patiently when I'm foolish enough to think I can do everything myself. You never tire of forgiving me and instead of annihilating me for offending You, You forgive me over and over again. You protect me from harm when I walk the way angels fear to tread, and You defend me before the Enemy of all mankind. Let me be as faithful to You, Lord God, as You are to me and let me be a true friend to everyone I meet.   *Mother Angelica*

O Lord, You are all merciful; take away my sins from me, and enkindle within me the fire of Your Holy Spirit. Take away this heart of stone and give me a heart of flesh and blood, a heart to love and adore You, a heart which may delight in You, love You and please You, for Jesus' sake. Amen.   *St. Ambrose*

My soul and body are defiled with many sinful deeds. My tongue and heart have run their course without restraint, God of gracious kindness, while I tremble before Your majesty; wretch that I am, trapped in my own insufficiency, I still look to You, the source of mercy. I hasten to You to be healed and to seek refuge under Your protection. I yearn to have You for my Savior for I cannot stand before You as my judge.

Lord, I show You my wounds and uncover my shame before You. My many great sins are known to me and they make me afraid. But I hope in Your mercy which knows no limits. Turn Your merciful gaze toward me, Lord Jesus Christ, eternal King, God and man crucified for mankind. Hear my cry of hope. Pity one so full of sin and wretchedness, for You are the inexhaustible fountain of forgiveness.   *St. Ambrose*

The confession of evil works is the beginning of good works.   *St. Augustine of Hippo*

Well, my poor heart, here we are,
fallen into the ditch which we
had made so firm a resolution to avoid;
Oh! let us rise and leave it forever.
Courage! henceforth, let us be more on our guard. God
will help us, we shall do well enough!   *St. Francis de Sales*

Where there is Love and Wisdom,
    there is neither Fear nor Ignorance.
Where there is Patience and Humility,
    there is neither Anger nor Annoyance.
Where there is Poverty and Joy,
    there is neither Cupidity nor Avarice.
Where there is Peace and Contemplation,

there is neither Care nor Restlessness.
Where there is the Fear of God to guard the dwelling,
   there no enemy can enter.
Where there is Mercy and Prudence,
   there is neither Excess nor Harshness.

St. Francis of Assisi

SEVEN

Waiting on God to Answer Your Prayers

Let the words of my mouth and the meditation of my
    heart
    be acceptable in thy sight,
    O LORD, my rock and my redeemer.   *Psalm 19:14*

My soul drew near to death,
    and my life was very near to Hades beneath.
They surrounded me on every side,
    and there was no one to help me;
I looked for the assistance of men,
    and there was none.
Then I remembered thy mercy, O Lord,
    and thy work from of old,
that thou dost deliver those who wait for thee
    and dost save them from the hand of their enemies.
And I sent up my supplication from the earth,
    and prayed for deliverance from death.
I appealed to the Lord, the Father of my lord,

not to forsake me in the days of affliction,
    at the time when there is no help against the proud.
I will praise thy name continually,
    and will sing praise with thanksgiving.
My prayer was heard,
    for thou didst save me from destruction
    and rescue me from an evil plight.
Therefore I will give thanks to thee and praise thee
    and will bless the name of the Lord.   *Sirach 51:6b-12*

"Ask, and it will be given you; seek, and you will find;
knock, and it will be opened to you. For every one who
asks receives, and he who seeks finds, and to him who
knocks it will be opened. Or what man of you, if his son
asks him for bread, will give him a stone? Or if he asks
for a fish, will give him a serpent? If you then, who are
evil, know how to give good gifts to your children, how
much more will your Father who is in heaven give good
things to those who ask him!"   *Matthew 7:7-11*

Lord, help us to grow in love for you and in trust of your
care and concern for us. Teach us to pray "in your
name," according to your character, and to rejoice in
the answer you give us—yes, no, wait, grow—as a sign
of your fatherly love for us.   *John Guest*

I asked God for strength,
that I might achieve . . .
I was made weak,

that I might learn humbly to obey.
I asked for health,
that I might do greater things . . .
I was given infirmity,
that I might do better things.
I asked for riches,
that I might be happy . . .
I was given poverty,
that I might be wise.
I asked for power,
that I might have the praise of men . . .
I was given weakness,
that I might feel the need of God.
I asked for all things,
that I might enjoy life . . .
I was given life,
that I might enjoy all things.
I got nothing that I asked for,
but everything I had hoped for.
Almost despite myself,
my unspoken prayers were answered.
I am among all men, most richly blessed!   *Anonymous*

God, teach me to be patient—
Teach me to go slow—
Teach me how to "wait on You"
When my way I do not know . . .
Teach me sweet forbearance
When things do not go right

So I remain unruffled
When others grow uptight . . .
Teach me how to quiet
My racing, rising heart
So I may hear the answer
You are trying to impart . . .
Teach me to let go, dear God,
And pray undisturbed until
My heart is filled with inner peace
And I learn to know Your will.   *Helen Steiner Rice*

After I enter the chapel, I place myself in the presence of God and I say to Him: "Lord, here I am; give me whatever you wish." If he gives me something, then I'm happy and I thank him. If he does not give me anything, then I thank him nonetheless, knowing that I deserve nothing. Then I begin to tell him of all that concerns me, my joys, my thoughts, my distress, and finally, I listen to him.   *St. Catherine Laboure*

To pray generously is not enough; we must pray devoutly, with fervor and piety. We must pray perseveringly and with great love.   *Mother Teresa of Calcutta*

EIGHT

For Times of Grieving and Loss

How long, O LORD? Wilt thou forget me for ever?
  How long wilt thou hide thy face from me?
How long must I bear pain in my soul,
  and have sorrow in my heart all the day?
How long shall my enemy be exalted over me?
Consider and answer me, O LORD my God; . . .

Psalm 13:1-3a

"Naked I came from my mother's womb, and naked
shall I return; the LORD gave, and the LORD has taken
away; blessed be the name of the Lord."   *Job 1:21*

But the souls of the righteous are in the hand of God,
  and no torment will ever touch them.
In the eyes of the foolish they seemed to have died,
  and their departure was thought to be an affliction,
  and their going from us to be their destruction;
but they are at peace.

179

For though in the sight of men they were punished,
   their hope is full of immortality.
Having been disciplined a little, they will receive great
     good,
   because God tested them
   and found them worthy of himself;
like gold in the furnace he tried them,
   and like a sacrificial burnt offering he accepted them.
In the time of their visitation they will shine forth,
   and will run like sparks through the stubble.
They will govern nations and rule over peoples,
   and the Lord will reign over them for ever.
Those who trust in him will understand truth,
   and the faithful will abide with him in love,
because grace and mercy are upon his elect,
   and he watches over his holy ones.   *Wisdom 3:1-9*

Jesus said to her, "I am the resurrection and the life; he
who believes in me, though he die, yet shall he live, and
whoever lives and believes in me shall never die. Do
you believe this?"   *John 11:25-26*

Jesus, my Lord,
Come to me,
Comfort me, console me.
Visit the hearts
In strange lands
yearning for you.
Visit the dying and those

Who have died without you.
Jesus, my Lord,
visit also those
Who persecute you.
Lord Jesus, you are my light
In the darkness.
You are my warmth
In the cold.
You are my happiness
In sorrow . . .
Amen. *Anonymous*

O God, source of our freedom and our unity,
whose Word made flesh announces
truth and peace in my life
if I do but keep his Commandments:
If I am in sickness, my sickness may serve him,
in my perplexity, may I serve him;
if I am in sorrow, my sorrow may serve him.
He does nothing in vain.
He knows what he is about.
He may take away my friends,
he may throw me among strangers,
he may make me feel desolate,
make my spirits sink,
hide my future from me—
still he knows what he is about.
Therefore, I will trust him. *John Henry Cardinal Newman*

Help us, O Lord, to know that as we give our loved one into thy hands, we give also into thy heart all our love and sorrow, and our penitence for whatever more we might have done in this earthly life. We pray thee to forgive us as we have forgiven each other; to keep alive and true in us our mutual love; and finally to bring us face to face with thy glory, thy loving presence among us all, according to the promise of thy blessed Son, our Saviour Jesus Christ.   *Unknown*

O Man of sorrows, and acquainted with grief, who knowest the depth of human pain, grant us grace to read our tragedies in the context of eternal love. Help us to know, even when we cannot understand, that in all things the Father worketh for good with those who love him; and teach us to do our part. Help us to realize that though the price of human love is the risk of loss, only through the love of those we have seen may we understand how to love him whom we have not seen. Grant that through our sorrow we may see more deeply into the hearts of all who suffer; and strengthen our hands to help. Finally, O Lord, open our eyes to behold the reality of the world unseen, where live the blessed dead in thy companionship.   *Charles T. Webb*

O holy and loving Father, Whose mercies are from everlasting to everlasting, we thank Thee that Thy children can flee for refuge in their afflictions to the blessed certainty of Thy love. From every grief that burdens our spirits, from the sense of solitude and loss, from the doubt and fainting of the soul in its trouble, we turn to Thee. Thou knowest our frame, Thou rememberest that we are dust. Be Thou our Strength and Deliverer; in our great need be Thou our Helper; pour Thy consolations into our hearts, and let the gospel of Thy beloved Son minister comfort and peace to our souls. Amen.   *Henry W. Foote*

When God takes someone from us, it is always for a good reason. When the sheep have grazed and thinned the grass in the lower regions, the shepherd will take a little lamb in his arms, carry it up the mountain where the grass is green, lay it down, and soon the other sheep will follow.

Every now and then our Lord takes a lamb from the parched field of a family up to those Heavenly Green Pastures, that the rest of the family may keep their eyes on their true home and follow through.   *Fulton Sheen*

NINE

For Consolation and Comfort

Blessed be the God and Father of our Lord Jesus Christ, the Father of mercies and God of all comfort, who comforts us in all our affliction, so that we may be able to comfort those who are in any affliction, with the comfort with which we ourselves are comforted by God. For as we share abundantly in Christ's sufferings, so through Christ we share abundantly in comfort too.   *2 Corinthians 1:3-5*

For thou art the God in whom I take refuge;
 why hast thou cast me off?
Why go I mourning
 because of the oppression of the enemy?
Oh send out thy light and thy truth;
 let them lead me,
let them bring me to thy holy hill
 and to thy dwelling!   *Psalm 43:2-3*

Thou hast kept count of my tossings;
   put thou my tears in thy bottle!
   Are they not in thy book?
Then my enemies will be turned back
   in the day when I call.
   This I know, that God is for me.
In God, whose word I praise,
   in the LORD, whose word I praise,
in God I trust without a fear.
   What can man do to me?   *Psalm 56:8-11*

Be thou my vision, O Lord of my heart,
Be all else but naught to me, save that thou art;
Be thou my best thought in the day and the night,
Both waking and sleeping, thy presence my light.
Be thou my wisdom, be thou my true word,
Be thou ever with me, and I with thee, Lord;
Be thou my great Father, and I thy true son;
Be thou in me dwelling, and I with thee one.
Be thou my breastplate, my sword for the fight;
Be thou my whole armour, be thou my true might;
Be thou my soul's shelter, be thou my strong tower;
O raise thou me heavenward, great power of my
   power.
Riches I heed not, nor man's empty praise;
Be thou mine inheritance now and always;
Be thou and thou only the first in my heart;
O sovereign of heaven, my treasure thou art.
High king of heaven, thou heaven's bright sun

O grant me its joys after vict'ry is won;
Great heart of my own heart, whatever befall,
Still be thou my vision, O ruler of all.   *Celtic Prayer*

Lord Jesus, today we accept from your merciful hands
what is to come. The times of trial in this world, the
suffering of our death, the sorrow and loneliness of our
last hours upon earth, the purifying, the unknown
pains of our purgatory. Into your hands, O Lord, into
your hands, we commit our living and dying, knowing
that you are the dawn of eternal day, the burning light
of the morning star.   *Caryll Houselander*

Since I belong to thee, my Savior, God,
All must be well, however rough my road;
However dark my way or prospects be,
All, all is right, since overruled by thee.
Feeblest of all thy flock, thou knowest me, Lord;
Helpless and weak, I stay upon thy word;
In all my weakness, this is still my plea,
That thou art mine, and I belong to thee.
Then come whatever may, I am secure,
Thy love unchanged shall to the end endure;
Frail though I am, thine everlasting arm
Shall shield thy child from every breath of harm.
                              Hannah Whitall Smith

The Father's way
   is always good,

and even if it should
    hurt you,
it will serve
    for your healing.
The one who is precious
    and truly of worth,
is tested through trouble
    and sorrow—
only in this way
    will you arrive
at the heavenly goal.   *Basilea Schlink*

Poverty and sorrow—well, with God's blessing, you, too, shall be changed into dearest friends. . . .

All in our God, whether cloudy or clear, that is our comfort. The world or anything in it can neither give or take.   *Elizabeth Seton*

All shall be well, and all shall be well, and all manner of things shall be well.   *Julian of Norwich*

TEN

For Overcoming Temptation and Sin

Moreover by them is thy servant warned;
  in keeping them there is great reward.
But who can discern his errors?
  Clear thou me from hidden faults.
Keep back thy servant also from presumptuous sins;
  let them not have dominion over me!
Then I shall be blameless,
  and innocent of great transgression.   *Psalm 19:11-13*

But thou, our God, art kind and true,
  patient, and ruling all things in mercy.
For even if we sin we are thine, knowing thy power;
  but we will not sin, because we know that we are
    accounted thine.
For to know thee is complete righteousness,
  and to know thy power is the root of immortality.
                        Wisdom 15:1-3

O that a guard were set over my mouth,
   and a seal of prudence upon my lips,
that it may keep me from falling,
   so that my tongue may not destroy me!
O Lord, Father and Ruler of my life,
   do not abandon me to their counsel,
   and let me not fall because of them!
O that whips were set over my thoughts,
   and the discipline of wisdom over my mind!
That they may not spare me in my errors,
   and that it may not pass by my sins;
in order that my mistakes may not be multiplied,
   and my sins may not abound;
then I will not fall before my adversaries,
   and my enemy will not rejoice over me.
O Lord, Father and God of my life,
   do not give me haughty eyes,
   and remove from me evil desire,
Let neither gluttony nor lust overcome me,
   and do not surrender me to a shameless soul.

                        Sirach 22:27; 23:1-6

No temptation has overtaken you that is not common to man. God is faithful, and he will not let you be tempted beyond your strength, but with the temptation will also provide the way of escape, that you may be able to endure it.   *1 Corinthians 10:13*

Fortify me with the grace of Your Holy Spirit and give Your peace to my soul that I may be free from all needless anxiety, solicitude and worry. Help me to desire always that which is pleasing and acceptable to You so that Your will may be my will.

Grant that I may rid myself of all unholy desires and that, for Your love, I may remain obscure and unknown in this world, to be known only to You. Do not permit me to attribute to myself the good that You perform in me and through me, but rather, referring all honor to Your Majesty, may I glory only in my infirmities, so that renouncing sincerely all vainglory which comes from the world, I may aspire to that true and lasting glory which comes from You. Amen.   *St. Frances Xavier Cabrini*

Give us, Lord, a humble, quiet, peaceable, patient, tender and charitable mind, and in all our thoughts, words and deeds a taste of the Holy Spirit. Give us, Lord, a lively faith, a firm hope, a fervent charity, a love of you. Take from us all lukewarmness in meditation, dullness in prayer. Give us fervour and delight in thinking of you and your grace, your tender compassion towards me. The things that we pray for, good Lord, give us grace to labour for: through Jesus Christ our Lord.   *St. Thomas More*

Grant us, O Lord, to pass this day in gladness and peace, without stumbling and without stain; that, reaching the eventide victorious over all temptations, we may praise you, the eternal God, who are blessed, and governs all things, world without end. Amen.

Mozarabic Liturgy

O Holy Angel, that keepest guard over my despondent soul and passionate life, leave me not, a sinner, nor depart from me to my undoing; grant not a place to the crafty enemy to overcome me by the force of this mortal body; strengthen my weak and feeble hand, and set me on the path of salvation. Yea, holy Angel of God, guardian and protector of my hopeless body and soul, forgive me everything wherein I have offended thee every day of my life, and what I have done amiss this past night; protect me during the present day, and preserve me from every attempt of the enemy. May I not anger God by any sin. Pray for me to the Lord, that he may establish me in his fear, and prove me a servant worthy of his kindness. Amen.   *Anonymous*

Help me, Lord,
or I shall perish.
Lord Jesus, stiller of storms,
bring peace to my soul.
Lord Jesus, I want to please thee
rather than to sin;
and if I do not feel that I want
to please thee, give me the grace
to want to please thee.

I want to want to please thee . . .
and I do not want to sin.   *Hubert von Zeller, OSB*

Our Lord permits us to fail in little occasions, that we
may humble ourselves and know that if we overcome
certain great temptations, it is not by our own strength.
                                    St. Francis de Sales

ELEVEN

For Receiving God's Forgiveness

"I know that thou canst do all things,
   and that no purpose of thine can be thwarted.
'Who is this that hides counsel without knowledge?'
Therefore I have uttered what I did not understand,
   things too wonderful for me, which I did not know.
'Hear, and I will speak;
   I will question you, and you declare to me.'
I had heard of thee by the hearing of the ear,
   but now my eye sees thee;
therefore I despise myself,
   and repent in dust and ashes."   *Job 42:2-6*

"To the Lord our God belong mercy and forgiveness; because we have rebelled against him, and have not obeyed the voice of the Lord our God by following his laws, which he set before us by his servants the prophets. . . .

"O my God, incline thy ear and hear; open thy eyes

and behold our desolations, and the city which is called
by thy name; for we do not present our supplications
before thee on the ground of our righteousness, but on
the ground of thy great mercy. O Lord, hear; O Lord,
forgive; O Lord, give heed and act; delay not, for thy
own sake, O my God, because thy city and thy people
are called by thy name!'' *Daniel 9:9-10, 18-19*

All their works are as the sun before him,
   and his eyes are continually upon their ways.
Their iniquities are not hidden from him,
   and all their sins are before the Lord.
A man's almsgiving is like a signet with the Lord,
   and he will keep a person's kindness like the apple of
      his eye.
Afterward he will arise and requite them,
   and he will bring their recompense on their heads.
Yet on those who repent he grants a return,
   and he encourages those whose endurance is failing.
                                             Sirach 17:19-24

O Lord, the house of my soul is narrow;
enlarge it, that you may enter in.
It is in ruins, please repair it.
It is displeasing to you; I know and acknowledge it.
But to whom can I call for help, to clear and
repair it, but you?
Cleanse me from my secret faults, O Lord,
and spare your servant. *St. Augustine of Hippo*

O Lord, who hast mercy upon all, take away from me my sins, and mercifully kindle in me the fire of Thy Holy Spirit. Take away from me the heart of stone, and give me a heart of flesh, a heart to love and adore Thee, a heart to delight in Thee, to follow and to enjoy Thee, for Christ's sake.   *St. Ambrose of Milan*

O God, though our sins be seven, though our sins be seventy times seven, though our sins be more in number than the hairs of our head, yet give us grace in loving penitence to cast ourselves down into the depths of your Compassion.   *Christina Rossetti*

Forgive us, O Lord,
For everything that has spoiled our home life:
For the moodiness and irritability which made us
    difficult to live with;
For the insensitiveness which made us careless of the
    feelings of others;
For selfishness which made life harder for others.
Forgive us, O Lord,
For everything that has spoiled our witness for Thee;
That so often men would never have known that which
    we said with our lips;
For the difference between our creed and our conduct,
    our profession and our practice;
For any example which made it easier for men to
    criticise Thy church or for another to sin.

When we think of ourselves and of the meanness and ugliness and weakness of our lives, we thank Thee for Jesus Christ our Saviour. Grant unto us a true penitence for our sins. Grant that at the foot of the Cross, we may find our burdens rolled away. And so strengthen us by Thy Spirit that in the days to come, we may live more nearly as we ought. Through Jesus Christ our Lord. Amen.   *William Barclay*

Forgive me my sins, O Lord; forgive me the sins of my youth and the sins of my age, the sins of my soul and the sins of my body, my secret and my whispering sins, my presumptuous and my crying sins, the sins that I have done to please myself, and the sins that I have done to please others. Forgive me those sins which I know, and those which I know not; forgive them, O Lord, forgive them all of Thy great goodness.

Lancelot Andrews

No force can prevail with a Father like the tears of his child, nor is there anything which so moves God to grant us, not justice, but mercy, as our sorrow and self-accusation.   *John of Avila*

You have fallen down.
You are dirty.
You no longer dare to step
into God's presence.
He seems to be so far away from you.

But it is exactly now that the Father is waiting for you.
He waits for the child who has fallen
down, as a mother waits for her child
who has got dirty so that she can
wash him.
He wants to cleanse you in the blood of His son.
So come!   *Basilea Schlink*

Part IV

Lord, Lead Me to Everlasting Life

ONE

A Treasury of Catholic Prayers

A. GENERAL PRAYERS TO THE FATHER, THE SON AND THE HOLY SPIRIT.

The Sign of the Cross

In the name of the Father, and of the Son, and of the Holy Spirit. Amen.

The Apostles' Creed

I believe in God, the Father Almighty, creator of heaven and earth.
I believe in Jesus Christ, his only Son, our Lord.
He was conceived by the power of the Holy Spirit and born of the Virgin Mary.
He suffered under Pontius Pilate, was crucified, died, and was buried.
He descended to the dead.
On the third day he rose again.

He ascended into heaven, and is seated at the right hand of the Father.
He will come again to judge the living and the dead.
I believe in the Holy Spirit, the Holy Catholic Church, the communion of saints, the forgiveness of sins, the resurrection of the body, and the life everlasting. Amen.

The Lord's Prayer

Our Father, who art in heaven, hallowed be Thy name; Thy kingdom come; Thy will be done on earth as it is in heaven. Give us this day our daily bread; and forgive us our trespasses as we forgive those who trespass against us; and lead us not into temptation, but deliver us from evil. Amen.

Glory Be to the Father or the Doxology

Glory be to the Father, and to the Son, and to the Holy Spirit. As it was in the beginning, is now, and ever shall be, world without end. Amen.

An Act of Faith

O my God, I firmly believe that You are one God in Three Divine Persons, Father, Son, and Holy Spirit; I believe that Your Divine Son became man and died for our sins, and that He will come to judge the living and the dead. I believe these and all truths which the Holy

Catholic Church teaches, because You revealed them, who can neither deceive nor be deceived.

An Act of Hope

O my God, relying on Your infinite goodness and promises, I hope to obtain pardon of my sins, the help of Your grace, and life everlasting, through the merits of Jesus Christ, my Lord and Redeemer.

An Act of Love

O my God, I love You above all things, with my whole heart and soul, because You are all-good and worthy of all love. I love my neighbor as myself for the love of You. I forgive all who have injured me, and I ask pardon of all whom I have injured.

The Divine Praises

Blessed be God.
Blessed be His Holy Name.
Blessed be Jesus Christ, true God and true man.
Blessed be the Name of Jesus.
Blessed be His Most Sacred Heart.
Blessed be Jesus in the Most Holy Sacrament of the Altar.
Blessed be the Holy Spirit, the Paraclete.
Blessed be the great Mother of God, Mary most holy.
Blessed be her holy and Immaculate Conception.

Blessed be her glorious Assumption.
Blessed be the name of Mary, Virgin and Mother.
Blessed be St. Joseph, her most chaste spouse.
Blessed be God in His angels and in His Saints.
May the heart of Jesus, in the Most Blessed Sacrament,
be praised, adored, and loved with grateful affection, at
every moment, in all the tabernacles of the world, even
to the end of time. Amen.

Te Deum

You are God—we praise You;
You are the Lord—we acclaim You;
You are the eternal Father:
All creation worships You.
To You all the angels of Heaven and all the powers,
Cherubim and Seraphim, sing in endless praise—
   Holy, holy, holy, Lord, God of power and might,
   heaven and earth are full of Your glory.
The glorious company of apostles praise You;
The noble fellowship of the prophets praise You;
The white-robed army of martyrs praise You,
Throughout the world Holy Church acclaims You:
   Father of majesty unbounded,
   Your true and only Son, worthy of all worship,
   And the Holy Spirit, advocate and guide.
You, O Christ, are the king of glory,
The eternal Son of the Father.
When You became man to set us free, You did not

spurn the virgin's womb.

You overcame the sting of death and opened the kingdom of heaven to all believers.

You are seated at God's right hand in robes of glory.

We believe that You will come to be our Judge.

Come then, Lord, and help Your people bought with the price of Your own Precious Blood, and bring us with Your saints to glory everlasting.　*St. Nicetas*

Praises of the Lord God Most High

You are the holy Lord, the only God, who work wonders.

You are strong. You are great. You are most high.

You are the Almighty King, you, O Holy Father, King of heaven and earth,

You are three and one, the Lord God of gods;

You are good, all good, the highest good,

Lord God, living and true. You are love, charity.

You are wisdom, you are humility,

You are patience, you are beauty.

You are meekness, you are security.

You are quietude, you are joy.

You are our hope and gladness.

You are justice, you are temperance.

You are all our riches to the full.

You are beauty, you are meekness.

You are protector, you are our guardian and defender;

You are strength, you are refreshment.

You are our hope, you are our faith,
You are our charity; you are all our delight.
You are our eternal life:
The great and wondrous Lord,
God Almighty, merciful Savior!   *St. Francis*

Benedictus

Blessed be the Lord, the God of Israel,
   for he has visited and brought redemption to his
      people.
He has raised up a horn for our salvation
   within the house of David his servant,
even as he promised through the mouth of his holy
      prophets from of old:
   salvation from our enemies and from the hand of all
      who hate us,
to show mercy to our fathers
   and to be mindful of his holy covenant
and of the oath he swore to Abraham our father
   and to grant us that, rescued from the hand of
      enemies,
without fear we might worship him in holiness and
      righteousness
   before him all our days.
And you, child, will be called prophet of the Most High,
   for you will go before the Lord to prepare his ways,
to give his people knowledge of salvation

through the forgiveness of their sins,
because of the tender mercy of our God
  by which the daybreak from on high will visit us
to shine on those who sit in darkness and death's
     shadow
  to guide our feet into the path of peace.   *Luke 1:69-79*

Prayer Before a Crucifix

My good and dear Jesus,
I kneel before you,
asking you most earnestly
to engrave upon my heart
a deep and lively faith, hope and charity,
with true repentance for my sins
and a firm resolve to make amends.
As I reflect upon your five wounds,
and dwell upon them with deep compassion and grief,
I recall, good Jesus, the words the prophet David spoke
long ago concerning yourself;
they have pierced my hands and my feet,
they have counted all my bones!

Suscipe

Lord Jesus Christ,
take all my freedom,
my memory, my understanding, and my will.
All that I have and cherish
you have given me.

I surrender it all to be guided by your will.
Your grace and your love
are wealth enough for me.
Give me these, Lord Jesus,
and I ask for nothing more.

Peace Prayer of St. Francis

Lord, make me an instrument of your peace;
where there is hatred, let me sow love;
where there is injury, pardon;
where there is doubt, faith;
where there is despair, hope;
where there is darkness, light;
and where there is sadness, joy.
Grant that I may not so much seek
to be consoled as to console;
to be understood, as to understand,
to be loved as to love;
for it is in giving that we receive,
it is in pardoning that we are pardoned,
and it is in dying that we are born to eternal life.

A Prayer to the Holy Spirit

Come, Holy Spirit,
   fill my heart with Your holy gifts.
Let my weakness be penetrated with Your strength
this very day that I may fulfill all the duties of my state
conscientiously, that I may do what is right and just.

Let my charity be such as to offend no one, and hurt no one's feelings; so generous as to pardon sincerely any wrong done to me.

Assist me, O Holy Spirit, in all my trials of life, enlighten me in my ignorance, advise me in my doubts, strengthen me in my weakness, help me in all my needs, protect me in temptations and console me in afflictions.

Graciously hear me, O Holy Spirit, and pour Your light into my heart, my soul, and my mind.

Assist me to live a holy life and to grow in goodness and grace. Amen.

Holy Spirit Prayer of St. Augustine

Breathe in me, O Holy Spirit,
That my thoughts may all be holy;
Act in me, O Holy Spirit.
That my work, too, may be holy;
Draw my heart, O Holy Spirit,
That I love but what is holy.
Strengthen me, O Holy Spirit,
To defend all that is holy;
Guard me, then, O Holy Spirit,
That I always may be holy.

Come, Holy Spirit, fill the hearts of your faithful, and enkindle in them the fire of your love.
Send forth your Spirit and they shall be created.
And you shall renew the face of the earth.

Let us pray: O God, who has taught the hearts of the
faithful by the light of the Holy Spirit, grant that by the
gift of the same Spirit we may be always truly wise and
ever rejoice in his consolation. Amen.

Spirit of the living God,
fall afresh on me.
Break me, melt me,
mould me, fill me.
Spirit of the living God,
fall afresh on me.

Veni Creator Espiritus

Come, Holy Ghost, Creator, come
From thy bright heavenly throne,
Come, take possession of our souls,
And make them all thine own.
Thou who art called the Paraclete,
Best gift of God above,
The living spring, the living fire,
Sweet unction and true love.
Thou who are sev'nfold in thy grace,
Finger of God's right hand;
His promise, teaching little ones
To speak and understand.
O guide our minds with thy blest light,
With love our hearts inflame;
And with thy strength, which ne'er decays,

Confirm our mortal frame.
Far from us drive our deadly foe;
True peace unto us bring;
And through all perils lead us safe
Beneath thy sacred wing.
Through thee may we the Father know,
Through thee th'eternal Son,
And thee the Spirit of them both,
Thrice-blessed Three in One.
All glory to the Father be,
With his co-equal Son:
The same to thee, great Paraclete,
While endless ages run.   *Rabanus Maurus*

Veni Sancte Espiritus

Come, thou Holy Spirit
Send from highest heaven
Radiance of thy light.
Come, Father of the poor
Come, giver of all gifts
Come, light of every heart.
Of comforters the best
Come, light of every heart.
Of comforters the best
Dear guest of every soul
Refreshment ever sweet.
In our labors rest
Coolness in our heat

Comfort in our grief.
O most blessed light
Fill the inmost hearts
Of thy faithful ones.
Without thy holy presence
All is dark
Nothing free from sin.
What is soiled cleanse
What is dry refresh
What is wounded heal.
What is rigid bend
What is frozen warm
Guide what goes astray.
Give thy faithful ones
Who in thee confide
Sevenfold hallowing.
Give goodness its reward
Give journey safe through death
Give joy that has no end.   *translated by George Appleton*

B. PRAYERS TO THE BLESSED MOTHER

Hail Mary or Angelis Salutation

Hail Mary, full of grace,
the Lord is with you!
Blessed are you among women,

and blessed is the fruit of your womb, Jesus.
Holy Mary, Mother of God,
pray for us sinners,
now and at the hour of our death.
Amen.

The Angelus

Verse: The angel of the Lord declared unto Mary.
Response: And she conceived by the Holy Spirit. Hail
Mary . . .
Verse: Behold the handmaid of the Lord.
Response: Be it done unto me according to your word.
Hail Mary . . .
Verse: And the Word was made flesh.
Response: And dwelt among us. Hail Mary . . .
Verse: Pray for us, O holy Mother of God.
Response: That we may be made worthy of the
promises of Christ.
Let us pray. Pour forth, we beseech you, O Lord, your
grace into our hearts, that as we have known the
incarnation of Christ, your Son, by the message of an
angel, so by his passion and cross we may be brought to
the glory of his Resurrection. Through the same Christ
our Lord.

The Regina Coeli (Queen of Heaven)

Queen of heaven, rejoice, alleluia,
the Son you merited to bear, alleluia,

has risen as he said, alleluia,
Pray to God for us, alleluia.
Rejoice and be glad, O Virgin Mary, alleluia.
For the Lord has truly risen, alleluia.
God of life,
you have given joy to the world by the resurrection of
your Son, our Lord Jesus Christ. Through the prayers of
his mother, the Virgin Mary, bring us to the happiness
of eternal life. We ask this through Christ our Lord.
Amen.

Memorare

Remember, most loving Virgin Mary,
never was it heard
that anyone who turned to you for help
was left unaided.
Inspired by this confidence,
though burdened by my sins,
I run to your protection
for you are my mother.
Mother of the Word of God,
do not despise my words of pleading
but be merciful and hear my prayer.
Amen.

Hail Holy Queen or Salve Regina

Hail, holy Queen, Mother of mercy,
hail, our life, our sweetness, and our hope.

To you we cry, the children of Eve;
to you we send up our sighs,
mourning and weeping in this land of exile.
Turn, then, most gracious advocate,
your eyes of mercy toward us;
lead us home at last
and show us the blessed fruit of your womb, Jesus:
O clement, O loving, O sweet Virgin Mary.
Verse: Pray for us, O holy Mother of God.
Response: That we may be made worthy of the
promises of Christ.

Tota Pulchra

You are all fair, O Mary,
And the original stain is not in you.
You are the glory of Jerusalem,
The joy of Israel,
The honor of our people,
The advocate of sinners.
O Mary,
Virgin most prudent,
Mother most merciful,
Pray for us,
Intercede for us with our Lord Jesus Christ.

The Canticle of Mary

My soul proclaims the greatness of the Lord;
my spirit rejoices in God my savior.

For he has looked upon his handmaid's lowliness;
   behold, from now on will all ages call me blessed.
The Mighty One has done great things for me,
   and holy is his name.
His mercy is from age to age
   to those who fear him.
He has shown might with his arm,
   dispersed the arrogant of mind and heart.
He has thrown down the rulers from their thrones
   but lifted up the lowly.
The hungry he has filled with good things;
   the rich he has sent away empty.
He has helped Israel his servant,
   remembering his mercy,
according to his promise to our fathers,
   to Abraham and to his descendants forever.

Luke 1:46-55

C. PRAYERS FOR RECONCILIATION AND COMMUNION

The Confiteor or I Confess

I confess to almighty God,
and to you, my brothers and sisters,
that I have sinned through my own fault
in my thoughts and in my words,
in what I have done,

and in what I have failed to do;
and I ask blessed Mary, ever virgin,
all the angels and saints,
and you, my brothers and sisters,
to pray for me to the Lord our God.

A Prayer Before Confession

Come, Holy Spirit, into my soul.
Enlighten my mind that I may know the sins I ought to confess, and grant me Your grace to confess them fully, humbly and with contrite heart.
Help me to firmly resolve not to commit them again.
O Blessed Virgin, Mother of my Redeemer, mirror of innocence and sanctity, and refuge of penitent sinners, intercede for me through the Passion of Your Son, that I may obtain the grace to make a good confession.
All you blessed Angels and Saints of God, pray for me, a most miserable sinner, that I may repent from my evil ways, that my heart may henceforth be forever united with yours in eternal love. Amen.

A Prayer after Confession

My dearest Jesus,
I have told all my sins to the best of my ability. I have sincerely tried to make a good confession and I know that you have forgiven me. Thank you, dear Jesus!
Your divine heart is full of love and mercy for poor

sinners. I love You, dear Jesus; You are so good to me.
My loving Savior, I shall try to keep from sin and to love
You more each day.
Dearest Mother Mary,
Pray for me and help me to keep all of my promises.
Protect me and do not let me fall back into sin.
Dear God,
Help me to lead a good life. Without Your grace I can do
nothing. Amen.

An Act of Contrition

O my God, I am heartily sorry for having offended You.
I detest all my sins because I dread the loss of heaven
and the pains of hell.
But most of all because they offend You, my God, Who
are all good and deserving of all my love.
I firmly resolve, with the help of Your grace, to sin no
more and to avoid the near occasions of sin. Amen.

A Prayer for Spiritual Communion

I believe that You, O Jesus, are in the most holy
Sacrament. I love You and desire You. Come into my
heart. I embrace You. Oh, never leave me. May the
burning and most sweet power of Your love, O Lord
Jesus Christ, I beseech You, absorb my mind that I may
die through love of Your love, who were graciously
pleased to die through love of my love.   *St. Francis*

Prayer Before Communion

Come, O blessed Saviour, and nourish my soul with heavenly Food, the Food which contains every sweetness and every delight. Come, Bread of Angels, and satisfy the hunger of my soul. Come, glowing Furnace of Charity, and enkindle in my heart the flame of divine love. Come, Light of the World, and enlighten the darkness of my mind. Come, King of Kings, and make me obedient to Your holy will. Come, loving Saviour, and make me meek and humble.

Come, Friend of the Sick, and heal the infirmities of my body and the weakness of my soul. Come, Good Shepherd, my God and my All, and take me to Yourself. O most holy Mother, Mary Immaculate, prepare my heart to receive my Saviour.

Prayer After Holy Communion

Dear Lord, help me to remove from my mind every thought or opinion which You would not sanction, every feeling from my heart which You would not approve.

Grant that I may spend the hours of the day gladly working with You according to Your will.

Help me just for today and be with me in it. In the long hours of work, that I may not grow weary or slack in serving You.

In conversations that they may not be to me occasions of uncharitableness.

In the day's worries and disappointments, that I may be patient with myself and with those around me.

In moments of fatigue and illness, that I may be mindful of theirs rather than of myself.

In temptations, that I may be generous and loyal, so that when the day is over I may lay it at Your feet, with its successes which are all Yours, and its failures which are all my own, and feel that life is real and peaceful, and blessed when spent with you as the Guest of my soul. Amen.

Soul of Christ or Anima Christi

Soul of Christ sanctify me;
Body of Christ, save me;
Blood of Christ, inebriate me;
Water from the side of Christ, wash me;
Passion of Christ, strengthen me;
O Good Jesus, hear me;
Within Your wounds, hide me;
Never permit me to be separated from You;
From the wicked enemy, defend me;
In the hour of my death, call me
And bid me to come to Your side,
That with Your saints I may praise You,
For ever and ever. Amen.

D. PRAYERS FOR DAILY PROTECTION

Angel of God

Angel of God, my guardian dear, to whom His love entrusts me here, even this day be at my side to light and guard, to rule and guide. Amen.

Prayer to St. Michael

Saint Michael, the Archangel,
   defend us in battle,
Be our protection against the
   wickedness and snares of the devil;
May God rebuke him, we humbly
   pray and do thou,
O Prince of the heavenly host, by
   the power of God,
Thrust into hell Satan and
   all evil spirits who
Wander through the world
   for the ruin of souls. Amen.

St. Patrick's Breastplate

Christ be with me, Christ before me,
   Christ behind me,
Christ in me, Christ beneath me,
   Christ above me,

Christ on my right, Christ on my left,
Christ where I lie, Christ where I sit,
   Christ where I arise,
Christ in the heart of every man who thinks of me,
Christ in the mouth of every man who speaks of me,
Christ in every eye that sees me,
Christ in every ear that hears me.
   Salvation is of the Lord.
   Salvation is of the Lord,
   Salvation is of the Christ.
   May your salvation, O Lord, be ever with us.

E. MORNING PRAYERS

For God's Support

May the Lord support us
   all the day long
till the shadows lengthen
   and the evening comes,
and the busy world is hushed,
and the fever of life is over,
and our work is done!
Then in his mercy
may he give a safe lodging,
and a holy rest,
and peace at the last!   *John Henry Cardinal Newman*

Prayer of Dedication of the Twenty-Four Hours

O Lord, I give myself to you, I trust you wholly. You are wiser than I, more loving to me than I am to myself. Fulfill your high purpose in me whatever that be: work in me and through me. I am born to serve you, to be yours, to be your instrument. Let me turn my will over to you. I ask not to see, I ask not to know, I ask simply to be one with you in love.   *John Henry Cardinal Newman*

The Morning Offering

O Jesus, in union with your most Precious Blood poured out on the cross and offered in every Mass, I offer you today my prayers, works, joys, sorrows and sufferings for the praise of your Holy Name and all desires of your Sacred Heart; in reparation for sin, for the conversion of sinners, the union of all Christians and our final union with you in Heaven. Amen.

For Guidance

Lord God, King of heaven and earth,
be pleased this day
    to direct and make holy,
    to guide and govern,
    our hearts and bodies,
    our thoughts, words and deeds,
    in accord with your law,
    and the keeping of your commands;

that now and forever
we may, with your help,
be saved and set free;
Savior of the world,
who live and reign forever.   *Old Roman Breviary*

F. EVENING PRAYERS

An Evening Prayer

O my God, I thank you for all the benefits which I have ever received from you, and especially this day. Give me light to see what sins I have committed, and grant me grace to be truly sorry for them. Amen.

Be with us, Lord

Be with us, Lord, tonight. Stay to adore and praise, and give thanks for us while we sleep; to draw down mercy and grace upon the world: to give strength to the suffering souls in purgatory in their long night of waiting.

Stay with us, to ward off the anger of God from our crowded cities with their dens of vice, their crimes that call to Heaven for vengeance.

Stay with us, to guard the innocent, to sustain the tempted, to raise the fallen, to curb the power of the evil one, to prevent sin.

Stay with us, to comfort the sorrowing, to bless the death-beds, to grant contrition to the dying, to receive into the arms of Your mercy the thousands that this night must come before You for judgment.

O Good Shepherd, stay with Your sheep. Secure them against the perils that beset them. Stay, above all, with the suffering and dying. Grant us a quiet night and a perfect end. Be our merciful Shepherd to the last, that without fear we may appear before You as our Judge. Amen.

Watch, O Lord, with those who wake,
   or watch, or weep tonight,
   and give your angels and saints charge
   over those who sleep.
Tend your sick ones, O Lord Christ,
   Rest your weary ones,
   Bless your dying ones,
   Soothe your suffering ones,
   Shield your joyous ones,
   And all for your love's sake.   *St. Augustine*

A Prayer Before Sleeping

Save us, O Lord, while waking,
and guard us while sleeping,
That when we wake,
we may watch with Christ,
and when we sleep, we may rest in peace. Amen.

Nunc Dimittis

At last, all powerful Master, you give leave to your servant to go in peace, according to your promise. For my eyes have seen your salvation which you have prepared for all nations, the light to enlighten the Gentiles and give glory to Israel, your people. Give praise to the Father Almighty, to his Son, Jesus Christ, the Lord, to the Spirit, who dwells in our hearts, both now and forever. Amen.

G. PRAYERS FOR MEALTIMES

Prayer Before Meals

Bless us, O Lord, and these Your gifts, which we are about to receive from Your bounty, through Christ our Lord. Amen.

Prayer After Meals

We give You thanks for all Your benefits, almighty God, who live and reign forever; and may the souls of the faithful departed, through the mercy of God, rest in peace. Amen.

A Thanksgiving for God's Gifts and a Good Harvest

We plough the fields, and scatter
  The Good seed on the land,

But it is fed and watered
  By God's almighty hand:
He sends the snow in winter,
  The warmth to swell the grain,
The breezes, and the sunshine,
  And soft, refreshing rain.
  All good gifts around us
  Are sent from heaven above;
  Then thank the Lord, O thank the Lord,
  For all his love.

He only is the Maker
  Of all things near and far;
He paints the wayside flower,
  He lights the evening star;
The winds and waves obey him,
  By him the birds are fed;
Much more to us, his children,
  He gives our daily bread.

We thank thee then, O Father,
  For all things bright and good,
The seed-time and the harvest,
  Our life, our health, our food.
Accept the gifts we offer
  For all thy love imparts,
And, what thou most desirest,
  Our humble, thankful hearts.   *M. Claudius*

H. PRAYERS FOR OUR SERVICE

Teach us, good Lord,
to serve you as you deserve;
to give and not count the cost;
to fight and not heed the wounds;
to toil and not seek for rest;
to labor and not ask for reward
save that of knowing we do your will
through Jesus Christ our Lord.   *St. Ignatius*

I. PRAYERS FOR THE NEEDS OF OTHERS

Dear Jesus, Divine Physician and Healer of the Sick, we turn to You in this time of illness. O dearest Comforter of the troubled, alleviate our worry and sorrow with Your gentle love, and grant us the grace and strength to accept this burden. Dear God, we place our worries in Your hands. We place our sick under Your care and humbly ask that You restore Your servant to health again. Above all, grant us the grace to acknowledge Your holy will and know that whatsoever You do, You do for the love of us. Amen.

Prayer for the Dying

Most Merciful Jesus, lover of souls, I pray You, by the agony of Your most Sacred Heart, and by the sorrows of Your Immaculate Mother, to wash in Your Most Precious Blood, the sinners of the world who are now in their agony, and who will die today. Heart of Jesus, once in agony, have mercy on the dying. Amen.

Prayer for the Souls in Purgatory

O gentle Heart of Jesus, ever present in the Blessed Sacrament, ever consumed with burning love for the poor captive souls in Purgatory, have mercy on them. Be not severe in Your judgments, but let some drops of Your Precious Blood fall upon the devouring flames. And, Merciful Savior, send Your angels to conduct them to a place of refreshment, light and peace. Amen.

For Poor Souls

May the souls of the faithful departed, through the mercy of God, rest in peace. Amen.

Eternal Rest

Eternal rest grant to them, O Lord, and let perpetual light shine upon them. May they rest in peace. Amen.

J. PRAYERS FOR PERSONAL NEEDS

Lord Jesus, let me know myself and know You,
And desire nothing save only You.

Let me deny myself and love You.
Let me do everything for Your sake.
Let me humble myself and exalt You.
Let me think of nothing except of You.
Let me die to myself and live in You.
Let me accept whatever happens as from You.
Let me banish self and follow You,
And ever desire to follow You.
Let me fly from myself and take refuge in You,
that I may deserve to be defended by You.
Let me fear for myself, let me fear You,
And let me be among those who are chosen by You.
Let me distrust myself and put my trust in You.
Let me be willing to obey for Your sake.
Let me cling to nothing save only You,
And let me be poor because of You.
Look upon me that I may love You,
And forever enjoy You. Amen.   *St. Augustine*

Prayer for our Study

For God's Light
Creator of all things, true source of light and wisdom, lofty source of all being, graciously let a ray of your brilliance penetrate into the darkness of my understanding and take from me the double darkness in which I have been born: sin and ignorance.

Give me a sharp sense of understanding, a retentive memory, and the ability to grasp things correctly and fundamentally. Grant me the talent of being exact in my explanations, and the ability to express myself with thoroughness and charm.

Point out the beginning, direct the progress, help in the completion through Christ, our Lord.

St. Thomas Aquinas

TWO

Popular Catholic Devotions

A. THE HOLY ROSARY

How to say the Rosary

Introductory Prayers
 The Sign of the Cross
 The Apostles' Creed
 One Our Father
 Three Hail Marys
 One Glory Be

The Decades
 Announce the First mystery
 One Our Father
 Ten Hail Marys
 One Glory Be
 (Follow this sequence for the Second and for the remaining decades)

Concluding Prayers
   Hail, Holy Queen
   Let us Pray
   O God, whose only-begotten Son, by his life, death, and Resurrection, has purchased for us a reward of eternal salvation; grant, we beseech you, that meditating on these mysteries of the most holy rosary of the Blessed Virgin Mary, we may both imitate what they contain and obtain what they promise. Through the same Christ our Lord. Amen.
   Optional: The Litany of the Blessed Virgin Mary

The Mysteries of the Rosary

The Joyful Mysteries (Monday/Thursday)
1. The Annunciation (Luke 1:28-38)
2. The Visitation of Mary to Elizabeth (Luke 1:32-45)
3. The Nativity (Luke 2:6-7)
4. The Presentation of Jesus in the Temple (Luke 2: 22-24)
5. The Finding of Jesus in the Temple (Luke 2:46-52)

The Sorrowful Mysteries (Tuesday/Friday)
1. The Agony of Jesus in the Garden (Mark 14:32-36)
2. The Scourging at the Pillar (John 19:1)
3. The Crowning with Thorns (John 19:2)
4. The Carrying of the Cross (John 19:17)
5. The Crucifixion (Luke 23:33, 44-46)

The Glorious Mysteries (Wednesday/Saturday/Sunday)
1. The Resurrection of Jesus (Matthew 28:5-6)
2. The Ascension of Jesus into Heaven (Acts 1:6-12)
3. The Descent of the Holy Spirit upon the Apostles (Acts 2:1-4)
4. The Assumption of Mary into Heaven (Rev. 12:1)
5. The Coronation of Mary as Queen of Heaven (Rev. 12:1)

Themes for Meditation for Each Mystery

Joyful Mysteries: Spirit of Holy Joy

1. Annunciation	Humility
2. Visitation	Charity
3. Nativity	Poverty/Simplicity
4. Presentation	Obedience and Purity
5. The Finding of Jesus in the Temple	Piety

Sorrowful Mysteries: Spirit of Compassion, Contrition, and Reparation

1. Agony	Perseverance in prayer and contrition
2. Scourging	Penance
3. Crowning with Thorns	Moral Courage
4. Carrying of the Cross	Patience/Endurance
5. Crucifixion	Self-sacrifice for God and others/Forgiveness of injuries

Glorious Mysteries: Spirit of Adoration and Faith

1. Resurrection	Faith in and love of God
2. Ascension	Hope in God and for heaven
3. Descent of the Holy Spirit	The gifts of the Holy Spirit
4. Assumption	Devotion to Mary
5. Coronation of Mary	Perseverance until death; eternal happiness with God

B. THE WAY OF THE CROSS

Prayer before the Way

Jesus Christ, my Lord, with what great love you passed over the painful road which led you to death; and I, how often have I abandoned you. But now I love you with my whole soul, and because I love you, I am sincerely sorry for having offended you. My Jesus, pardon me, and permit me to accompany you in this journey. You are going to die for love of me, and it is my wish also to die for love of you.

Jesus, in your love I wish to live, in your love I wish to die.

First Station

Jesus is condemned to death
   This response is said before each station.

We adore you, Christ, and praise you.
Because by your holy cross you have redeemed the world.
Reading: Matthew 27:1-2, 11-14, 15-18, 20-26

Consider how Jesus, after having been scourged and crowned with thorns, was unjustly condemned by Pilate to die on the cross.

My loving Jesus, it was not Pilate; no, it was my sins that condemned you to die. I beseech you, by the merits of this sorrowful journey, to assist my soul in her journey towards eternity.

The following prayers and verse are said after each station.

I love you, Jesus, my love, above all things;
I repent with my whole heart for having offended you.
Never permit me to separate myself from you again.
Grant that I may love you always, then do with me what you will.
Our Father. Hail Mary. Glory be to the Father.

Second Station

Jesus receives the cross
We adore . . .
Reading: Mark 15:16-20

Consider how Jesus, in making this journey with the cross on his shoulders, thought of us, and offered for us to his Father the death he was about to undergo.

My Jesus, I embrace all the tribulations you have destined for me until death. I beseech you by the merits of the pain you suffered in carrying your cross, to give me the necessary help to carry mine with perfect patience and resignation.

I love you, Jesus . . . Our Father. Hail Mary. Glory be.

Third Station

Jesus falls the first time
We adore . . .
Reading: Isaiah 53:7-10

> Consider the first fall of Jesus under his cross. His flesh was torn by the scourges, his head was crowned with thorns; he had lost a great quantity of blood. So weakened he could scarcely walk, he yet had to carry this great load upon his shoulders. The soldiers struck him rudely, and he fell several times.

My Jesus, it is not the weight of the cross, but of my sins, which has made you suffer so much pain. By the merits of this first fall, deliver me from the misfortune of falling into mortal sin.

I love you, Jesus . . . Our Father. Hail Mary. Glory be.

Fourth Station

Jesus is met by his blessed mother
We adore . . .

Reading: John 19:25-27

> Consider the meeting of the Son and the mother, which took place on this journey. Their looks became like so many arrows to wound those hearts which loved each other so tenderly.

Jesus, by the sorrow you experienced in this meeting, grant me the grace of a truly devoted love for your most holy mother. And you, Mary, overwhelmed with sorrow, obtain for me by your intercession a continual and tender remembrance of the passion of your Son.

I love you, Jesus . . . Our Father. Hail Mary. Glory be.

Fifth Station

Simon of Cyrene helps Jesus to carry his cross
We adore . . .
Reading: Luke 23:26

> Consider how his cruel tormentors, seeing Jesus was on the point of expiring, and fearing he would die on the way, whereas they wished him to die the shameful death of the cross, constrained Simon of Cyrene to carry the cross behind our Lord.

Jesus, I will not refuse the cross, as the Cyrenian did; I accept it, I embrace it. I accept in particular, the death you have destined for me, with all the pains which may accompany it; I unite it to your death; I offer it to you.

You died for love of me; I will die for love of you. Help me by your grace.

I love you, Jesus . . . Our Father. Hail Mary. Glory be.

Sixth Station

Veronica wipes the face of Jesus
We adore . . .
Reading: Isaiah 53:2-9

> Consider how the holy woman named Veronica, seeing Jesus so ill-used, and his face bathed in sweat and blood, presented him with a towel, with which he wiped his adorable face, leaving on it the impression of his holy countenance.

Your face, Jesus, was beautiful before; but in this journey it has lost all its beauty, and wounds and blood have disfigured it. My soul also was once beautiful, when it received your grace in baptism; but I have disfigured it since by my sins. You alone, my redeemer, by your passion, can restore it to its former beauty.

I love you, Jesus . . . Our Father. Hail Mary. Glory be.

Seventh Station

Jesus falls the second time
We adore . . .

Reading Psalm 25: 16-17, 19-21

> Consider the second fall of Jesus under the cross; a fall which renews the pain of all the wounds in his head and members.

My most sweet Jesus, how many times have you pardoned me, and how many times have I fallen again, and begun again to offend you. By the merits of this second fall, give me the necessary help to persevere in your grace until death. Grant that in all temptations which assail me, I may always commend myself to you.

I love you, Jesus . . . Our Father. Hail Mary. Glory be.

Eighth Station

The women of Jerusalem mourn for our Lord
We adore . . .
Reading: Luke 23:27-28

> Consider how these women wept with compassion at seeing Jesus in such a pitiable state, streaming with blood, as he walked along. "Daughters of Jerusalem," said he, "weep not for me, but for yourselves and for your children."

My Jesus, laden with sorrows, I weep for the offences I have committed against you, because of the pains they have deserved, and still more because of the displeasure they have caused you, who has loved me so much. It is your love more than the fear of hell which causes me to weep for my sins.

I love you, Jesus . . . Our Father. Hail Mary. Glory be.

Ninth Station

Jesus falls for the third time
We adore . . .
Reading: Isaiah 53:7-9

Consider the third fall of Jesus Christ. His weakness was extreme, and the cruelty of his executioners excessive who tried to hasten his steps when he could scarcely move.

My outraged Jesus, by the merits of the weakness you suffered in going to Calvary, give me strength sufficient to conquer all human respect, and all my wicked passions, which have led me to reject your friendship.

I love you, Jesus . . . Our Father. Hail Mary. Glory be.

Tenth Station

Jesus is stripped of his garments
We adore . . .
Reading: Matthew 27:34-37

Consider the violence with which Jesus was stripped by the executioners. His inner garments adhered to his torn flesh, and they dragged them off so roughly that the skin came with them. Take pity on your Saviour thus cruelly treated.

My innocent Jesus, by the merits of the torments you felt, help me to strip myself of all affection to things of earth, in order that I may place all my love in you, who are so worthy of my love.

I love you, Jesus . . . Our Father. Hail Mary. Glory be.

Eleventh Station

Jesus is nailed to the cross
We adore . . .
Reading: Luke 23:33-38

> Consider how Jesus, having been placed upon the cross, extended his hands, and offered to his eternal Father the sacrifice of his life for our salvation. Those barbarians fastened him with nails, and then, securing the cross, allowed him to die with anguish on this infamous gibbet.

My Jesus, loaded with contempt, nail my heart to your feet, that it may ever remain there to love you and never quit you again.

I love you, Jesus . . . Our Father. Hail Mary. Glory be.

Twelfth Station

Jesus dies on the cross
We adore . . .

Reading: Luke 23:44-46

Consider how Jesus, being consumed with anguish after three hours' agony on the cross, abandoned himself to the weight of his body, bowed his head and died.

My dying Jesus, I kiss the cross on which you died for love of me. I have merited by my sins to die a miserable death. But your death is my hope. By the merits of your death, give me grace to die embracing your feet, and burning with love for you. I commit my soul into your hands.

I love you, Jesus . . . Our Father. Hail Mary. Glory be.

Thirteenth Station

Jesus is taken down from the cross
We adore . . .
Reading: Luke 23:50-52

Consider how, after our Lord had expired, two of his disciples, Joseph and Nicodemus, took him down from the cross and placed him in the arms of his afflicted mother, who received him with unutterable tenderness, and pressed him to her bosom.

Mother of sorrow, for the love of this Son, accept me for your servant, and pray for me. And my redeemer, since you have died for me, permit me to love you; for I wish but you, and nothing more.

I love you, Jesus . . . Our Father. Hail Mary. Glory be.

Fourteenth Station

Jesus is placed in the tomb
We adore . . .
Reading: Luke 23: 53-54

> Consider how the disciples carried the body of Jesus to bury it. Accompanied by his holy mother, who arranged it in the sepulchre with her own hands; they then closed the tomb, and all withdrew.

My buried Jesus, I kiss the stone that encloses you. But you rose again the third day. I beseech you by your resurrection, make me rise glorious with you at the last day, to be always united with you in heaven to praise you and love you for ever.

I love you, Jesus . . . Our Father. Hail Mary. Glory be.

Let us Pray.

Lord Jesus Christ, you walked the way to Calvary to rescue us from our sin, but the Father, pleased with your obedient submission to his will, glorified you in the resurrection. May we follow obediently in your footsteps so that one day we may share in the glory of your risen life. We make this prayer through you who live with the Father and Holy Spirit, one God for ever and ever. Amen.

THREE

Litanies

LITANY OF THE BLESSED VIRGIN

Lord, have mercy.
Christ, have mercy.
Lord, have mercy.
Christ, hear us.

Lord, have mercy.
Christ, have mercy.
Lord, have mercy.
Christ, graciously
  hear us.

God, the Father of Heaven,
God, the Son, Redeemer of
  the world,
God, the Holy Spirit,
Holy Trinity, one God,
Holy Mary,
Holy Mother of God,
Holy Virgin of virgins,
Mother of Christ,
Mother of divine grace,
Mother most pure,
Mother most chaste,
Mother inviolate,

have mercy on us.

have mercy on us.
have mercy on us.
have mercy on us.
pray for us.
pray for us.
pray for us.
pray for us.
pray for us.
pray for us.
pray for us.
pray for us.

Mother undefiled,	*pray for us.*
Mother most amiable,	*pray for us.*
Mother most admirable,	*pray for us.*
Mother of good counsel,	*pray for us.*
Mother of our Creator,	*pray for us.*
Mother of our Savior,	*pray for us.*
Virgin most prudent,	*pray for us.*
Virgin most venerable,	*pray for us.*
Virgin most renowned,	*pray for us.*
Virgin most powerful,	*pray for us.*
Virgin most merciful,	*pray for us.*
Virgin most faithful,	*pray for us.*
Mirror of justice,	*pray for us.*
Seat of Wisdom,	*pray for us.*
Cause of our joy,	*pray for us.*
Spiritual vessel,	*pray for us.*
Vessel of honor,	*pray for us.*
Vessel of singular devotion,	*pray for us.*
Mystical rose,	*pray for us.*
Tower of David,	*pray for us.*
Tower of ivory,	*pray for us.*
House of gold,	*pray for us.*
Ark of the covenant,	*pray for us.*
Gate of heaven,	*pray for us.*
Morning star,	*pray for us.*
Health of the sick,	*pray for us.*
Refuge of sinners,	*pray for us.*
Comforter of the afflicted,	*pray for us.*
Help of Christians,	*pray for us.*

Queen of angels,	*pray for us.*
Queen of Patriarchs,	*pray for us.*
Queen of Prophets,	*pray for us.*
Queen of Apostles,	*pray for us.*
Queen of Martyrs,	*pray for us.*
Queen of Confessors,	*pray for us.*
Queen of Virgins,	*pray for us.*
Queen of all Saints,	*pray for us.*
Queen conceived without original sin,	*pray for us.*
Queen assumed into heaven,	*pray for us.*
Queen of the most holy rosary,	*pray for us.*
Queen of peace,	*pray for us.*
Lamb of God, who takes away the sins of the world,	*spare us, O Lord.*
Lamb of God, who takes away the sins of the world,	*graciously hear us, O Lord.*
Lamb of God, who takes away the sins of the world,	*have mercy on us.*

Pray for us, O holy Mother of God.
That we may be made worthy of the promises of Christ,

Let us Pray
Grant, we beseech You, O Lord God, that we Your servants, may enjoy perpetual health of soul and body; and by the glorious intercession of blessed Mary, ever Virgin, may be delivered from present sorrows and rejoice in eternal happiness. Through Christ, our Lord. Amen.

LITANY OF THE SACRED HEART OF JESUS

Lord, have mercy on us.	*Lord, have mercy on us.*
Christ, have mercy on us.	*Christ, have mercy on us.*
Lord, have mercy on us.	*Lord, have mercy on us.*
Christ, hear us.	*Christ, graciously hear us.*
God the Father of heaven,	*have mercy on us.*
God the Holy Spirit,	*have mercy on us.*
Holy Trinity, one God,	*have mercy on us.*
Heart of Jesus, Son of the Eternal Father,	*have mercy on us.*
Heart of Jesus, formed by the Holy Spirit in the womb of the Virgin Mother,	*have mercy on us.*
Heart of Jesus, united substantially with the Word of God,	*have mercy on us.*
Heart of Jesus of infinite majesty,	*have mercy on us.*
Heart of Jesus, holy temple of God,	*have mercy on us.*
Heart of Jesus, tabernacle of the Most High,	*have mercy on us.*
Heart of Jesus, house of God and gate of heaven,	*have mercy on us.*
Heart of Jesus, glowing furnace of charity,	*have mercy on us.*
Heart of Jesus,	

vessel of justice and love, *have mercy on us.*
Heart of Jesus,
   full of goodness and love, *have mercy on us.*
Heart of Jesus, abyss of all virtues, *have mercy on us.*
Heart of Jesus,
   most worthy of all praise, *have mercy on us.*
Heart of Jesus,
   king and center of all hearts, *have mercy on us.*
Heart of Jesus,
   in whom are all the treasures of
   wisdom and knowledge, *have mercy on us.*
Heart of Jesus,
   in whom dwells all the fullness
   of divinity, *have mercy on us.*
Heart of Jesus,
   in whom the Father is well
   pleased, *have mercy on us.*
Heart of Jesus,
   in whose fullness we have all
   received, *have mercy on us.*
Heart of Jesus,
   desire of the eternal hills, *have mercy on us.*
Heart of Jesus,
   patient and rich in mercy, *have mercy on us.*
Heart of Jesus,
   rich to all who invoke You, *have mercy on us.*
Heart of Jesus,
   fount of life and holiness, *have mercy on us.*
Heart of Jesus,

propitiation for our sins,   *have mercy on us.*
Heart of Jesus,
    loaded down with opprobrium,   *have mercy on us.*
Heart of Jesus,
    bruised for our offenses,   *have mercy on us.*
Heart of Jesus,
    made obedient unto death,   *have mercy on us.*
Heart of Jesus,
    pierced with a lance,   *have mercy on us.*
Heart of Jesus,
    source of all consolation,   *have mercy on us.*
Heart of Jesus,
    our life and resurrection,   *have mercy on us.*
Heart of Jesus,
    our peace and reconciliation,   *have mercy on us.*
Heart of Jesus, victim for our sin,   *have mercy on us.*
Heart of Jesus,
    salvation of those who hope
    in You,   *have mercy on us.*
Heart of Jesus,
    hope of those who die in You,   *have mercy on us.*
Heart of Jesus,
    delight of all saints,   *have mercy on us.*
Lamb of God, who takes away
    the sins of the world,   *spare us, O Lord.*
Lamb of God, who takes away
    the sins of the world,   *spare us, O Lord.*
Lamb of God, who takes away   *graciously hear us,*
    the sins of the world,   *O Lord.*

Lamb of God, who takes away
  the sins of the world,   *have mercy on us.*
Jesus, meek and humble of heart,
Make our hearts like to Yours.

Let us Pray
Almighty and everlasting God, graciously regard the
heart of Your well-beloved Son and the acts of praise and
satisfaction which He renders You on behalf of us
sinners; and through their merit, grant pardon to us who
implore Your mercy, in the name of Your Son Jesus
Christ, Who lives and reigns with You in the unity of the
Holy Spirit, one God, world without end, Amen.

A SHORT LITANY OF THE SAINTS

Lord, have mercy on us.	*Lord, have mercy on us.*
Christ, have mercy on us.	*Christ, have mercy on us.*
Lord, have mercy on us.	*Lord, have mercy on us.*
Holy Mary, Mother of God,	*pray for us.*
St. Michael,	*pray for us.*
Holy angels of God,	*pray for us.*
St. Joseph,	*pray for us.*
St. John the Baptist,	*pray for us.*
St. Peter and St. Paul,	*pray for us.*
St. Andrew,	*pray for us.*
St. John,	*pray for us.*
St. Mary Magdalene,	*pray for us.*

St. Stephen,	*pray for us.*
St. Ignatius,	*pray for us.*
St. Lawrence,	*pray for us.*
St. Perpetua and St. Felicity,	*pray for us.*
St. Agnes,	*pray for us.*
St. Gregory,	*pray for us.*
St. Augustine,	*pray for us.*
St. Athanasius,	*pray for us.*
St. Basil,	*pray for us.*
St. Martin,	*pray for us.*
St. Benedict,	*pray for us.*
St. Francis and St. Dominic,	*pray for us.*
St. Francis Xavier,	*pray for us.*
St. John Vianney,	*pray for us.*
St. Catherine,	*pray for us.*
St. Theresa,	*pray for us.*
All you saints of God,	*pray for us.*
Lord, be merciful,	*Lord, save us,*
From all harm,	*Lord, save us,*
From every sin,	*Lord, save us,*
From all temptations,	*Lord, save us,*
From everlasting death,	*Lord, save us,*
By Your coming among us,	*Lord, save us,*
By Your death and rising to new life,	*Lord, save us,*
By Your gift of the Holy Spirit,	*Lord, save us,*
Be merciful to us sinners,	*Lord, hear our prayer.*
Guide and protect Your Holy	

Church,   *Lord, hear our prayer.*
Keep our Pope and all the
   Clergy in Faithful service
   to Your Church.   *Lord, hear our prayer.*
Bring all people together in
   trust and peace.   *Lord, hear our prayer.*
Strengthen us in Your service. *Lord, hear our prayer.*

A LONGER LITANY OF THE SAINTS

(Petition to God:)

Lord, have mercy.   *Lord, have mercy.*
Christ, have mercy.   *Christ, have mercy.*
Lord, have mercy.   *Lord, have mercy.*
God our father in heaven,   *have mercy on us.*
God the Son, our redeemer,   *have mercy on us.*
God the Holy Spirit,   *have mercy on us.*
Holy Trinity, one God,   *have mercy on us.*

(Petition to the saints:)

Holy Mary,   *pray for us.*
Mother of God,   *pray for us.*
Most honored of all women,   *pray for us.*
Michael, Gabriel, and Raphael, *pray for us.*
Angels of God,   *pray for us.*

(Prophets and fathers of our faith:)

Abraham, Moses, and Elijah,	*pray for us.*
St. Joseph,	*pray for us.*
St. John the Baptist,	*pray for us.*
Holy patriarchs and prophets,	*pray for us.*

(Apostles and followers of Christ:)

St. Peter and St. Paul,	*pray for us.*
St. Andrew,	*pray for us.*
St. John and St. James,	*pray for us.*
St. Thomas,	*pray for us.*
St. Matthew,	*pray for us.*
All holy apostles,	*pray for us.*
St. Luke,	*pray for us.*
St. Mark,	*pray for us.*
St. Barnabas,	*pray for us.*
St. Mary Magdalen,	*pray for us.*
All disciples of the Lord,	*pray for us.*

(All holy martyrs for Christ:)

St. Stephen,	*pray for us.*
St. Ignatius,	*pray for us.*
St. Polycarp,	*pray for us.*
St. Justin,	*pray for us.*
St. Paul Miki,	*pray for us.*
St. Isaac Jogues and	

St. John de Brebeuf,	*pray for us.*
St. Peter Chanel,	*pray for us.*
St. Charles Lwanga,	*pray for us.*
St. Maria Goretti,	*pray for us.*
St. Lawrence,	*pray for us.*
St. Cyprian,	*pray for us.*
St. Boniface,	*pray for us.*
St. Thomas Becket,	*pray for us.*
St. John Fisher and St. Thomas More,	*pray for us.*
St. Perpetua and St. Felicity,	*pray for us.*
St. Agnes,	*pray for us.*

(Bishops, doctors, and other holy persons:)

St. Leo and St. Gregory,	*pray for us.*
St. Ambrose,	*pray for us.*
St. Jerome,	*pray for us.*
St. Augustine,	*pray for us.*
St. Athanasius,	*pray for us.*
St. Basil and St. Gregory,	*pray for us.*
St. John Chrysostom,	*pray for us.*
St. Martin,	*pray for us.*
St. Patrick,	*pray for us.*
St. Cyril and St. Methodius,	*pray for us.*
St. Charles Borromeo,	*pray for us.*
St. Francis de Sales,	*pray for us.*
St. Anthony,	*pray for us.*
St. Pius,	*pray for us.*

St. Benedict,	*pray for us.*
St. Bernard,	*pray for us.*
St. Francis and St. Dominic,	*pray for us.*
St. Thomas Aquinas,	*pray for us.*
St. Ignatius Loyola,	*pray for us.*
St. Francis Xavier,	*pray for us.*
St. Vincent de Paul,	*pray for us.*
St. John Vianney,	*pray for us.*
St. John Bosco,	*pray for us.*
St. Teresa of Avila,	*pray for us.*
St. Rose,	*pray for us.*
All you saints of God,	*pray for us.*

(Petition for mercy:)

Lord, be merciful.	*Lord, save us.*
From all harm,	*Lord, save us.*
From every sin,	*Lord, save us.*
From all temptations,	*Lord, save us.*
From everlasting death,	*Lord, save us.*
By your coming among us,	*Lord, save us.*
By your death and rising to new life,	*Lord, save us.*
By your gift of the Holy Spirit,	*Lord, save us.*
Be merciful to us sinners, guide and protect your holy Church.	*Lord, hear our prayer.*
	Lord, hear our prayer.
Keep our pope and all the clergy in faithful service to	

your Church.	*Lord, hear our prayer.*
Bring all peoples together in trust and peace.	*Lord, hear our prayer.*
Strengthen us in your service.	*Lord, hear our prayer.*

(Holy men and women:)

St. Louis,	*pray for us.*
St. Monica,	*pray for us.*
St. Elizabeth,	*pray for us.*
All holy men and women,	*pray for us.*

(Petition to Christ:)

Lord, be merciful.	*Lord, save your people.*
From all evil,	*Lord, save your people.*
From every sin,	*Lord, save your people.*
From the snares of the devil,	*Lord, save your people.*
From anger and hatred,	*Lord, save your people.*
From every evil intention,	*Lord, save your people.*
From everlasting death,	*Lord, save your people.*
By your coming as man,	*Lord, save your people.*
By your birth,	*Lord, save your people.*
By your baptism and fasting,	*Lord, save your people.*
By your sufferings and cross,	*Lord, save your people.*
By your death and burial,	*Lord, save your people.*
By your rising to new life,	*Lord, save your people.*
By your return in glory to the Father,	*Lord, save your people.*
By your gift of the Holy Spirit,	*Lord, save your people.*

By your coming again in glory, *Lord, save your people.*
Christ, Son of the living God, *have mercy on us.*
You came into this world; *have mercy on us.*
You suffered for us on the
    cross; *have mercy on us.*
You died to save us; *have mercy on us.*
You lay in the tomb; *have mercy on us.*
You rose from the dead; *have mercy on us.*
You returned in glory to
    the Father; *have mercy on us.*
You sent the Holy Spirit upon
    your Apostles; *have mercy on us.*
You are seated at the right
    hand of the Father; *have mercy on us.*
You will come again to judge
    the living and the dead; *have mercy on us.*

(General petition:)

Lord, be merciful to us. *Lord, hear our prayer.*
Give us true repentance. *Lord, hear our prayer.*
Strengthen us in your service. *Lord, hear our prayer.*
Reward with eternal life all
    who do good to us. *Lord, hear our prayer.*
Bless the fruits of the earth
    and of our labor. *Lord, hear our prayer.*
Lord, show us your kindness. *Lord, hear our prayer.*
Raise our thoughts and desires
    to you. *Lord, hear our prayer.*

Save us from final damnation.	*Lord, hear our prayer.*
Save our friends and all who have helped us.	*Lord, hear our prayer.*
Grant eternal rest to all who have died in the faith.	*Lord, hear our prayer.*
Spare us from disease, hunger and war.	*Lord, hear our prayer.*
Deliver us from all undue anxiety.	*Lord, hear our prayer.*
Bring all peoples together in trust and peace.	*Lord, hear our prayer.*
Guide and protect your people.	*Lord, hear our prayer.*
Keep the pope and all religious and faithful clergy in service to your people.	*Lord, hear our prayer.*
Bring all together in unity.	*Lord, hear our prayer.*
Lead all to the light of the Gospel.	*Lord, hear our prayer.*

(Conclusion:)

Christ, hear us.	*Christ, hear us.*
Lord Jesus,	*hear our prayer.*
Lamb of God, you take away the sin of the world,	*have mercy on us.*
Lamb of God, you take away the sin of the world,	*spare us, O Lord.*
Lamb of God, you take away the sin of the world,	*graciously hear us, O Lord.*

Let us pray
Lord God, you have gathered together a people to show the vastness of your love. We humbly ask you to enable us to see your love in those who choose to serve you. Grant to all of us the overwhelming desire to do your will, and the goodness to admire those who do. Free us from guilt and fear so that we may be open to your good people everywhere. Help us to share and be open to those who share your love.

LITANY OF HUMILITY

O Jesus, meek and humble of heart,	*hear me.*
From the desire of being esteemed,	*deliver me, Lord Jesus.*
From the desire of being extolled,	*deliver me, Lord Jesus.*
From the desire of being honored,	*deliver me, Lord Jesus.*
From the desire of being praised,	*deliver me, Lord Jesus.*
From the desire of being preferred before others,	*deliver me, Lord Jesus.*
From the desire of being consulted,	*deliver me, Lord Jesus.*
From the desire of being approved,	*deliver me, Lord Jesus.*

From the desire of being
highly regarded,   *deliver me, Lord Jesus.*

From the fear of being
humiliated,   *deliver me, Lord Jesus.*

From the fear of being
rebuked,   *deliver me, Lord Jesus.*

From the fear of being
forgotten,   *deliver me, Lord Jesus.*

From the fear of being
wronged,   *deliver me, Lord Jesus.*

From the fear of being
suspected,   *deliver me, Lord Jesus.*

That others may be loved more   *Jesus, grant me the*
than I,   *grace to desire it.*

That in the opinion of the
world, others may increase   *Jesus, grant me the*
and I decrease,   *grace to desire it.*

That others may be chosen and   *Jesus, grant me the*
I passed over,   *grace to desire it.*

That others be praised and I go   *Jesus, grant me the*
unnoticed,   *grace to desire it.*

That others should be
preferred before me in   *Jesus, grant me the*
everything,   *grace to desire it.*

That others may become holier
than I, provided that I may   *Jesus, grant me the*
become as holy as I should,   *grace to desire it.*

Cardinal Rafael Merry del Val

FOUR

A Guide to a Good Examination of Conscience

THE TEN COMMANDMENTS

1. I am the Lord your God; you shall not have strange gods before Me.
2. You shall not take the name of the Lord your God in vain.
3. Remember to keep holy the Lord's day.
4. Honor your father and your mother.
5. You shall not kill.
6. You shall not commit adultery.
7. You shall not steal.
8. You shall not bear false witness against your neighbor.
9. You shall not covet your neighbor's wife.
10. You shall not covet your neighbor's goods.

THE BEATITUDES (Matthew 5:3-11)

Blessed are the poor in spirit,
 for theirs is the kingdom of heaven.
Blessed are the meek,
 for they shall possess the earth.
Blessed are they who mourn,
 for they shall be comforted.
Blessed are they who hunger and thirst for justice,
 for they shall be satisfied.
Blessed are the merciful,
 for they shall obtain mercy.
Blessed are the clean of heart,
 for they shall see God.
Blessed are the peacemakers,
 for they shall be called children of God.
Blessed are they who suffer persecution for justice'
 sake,
 for theirs is the kingdom of heaven.
Blessed are you when men reproach you, and
 persecute you, and
 speaking falsely, say all manner of evil
 against you, for My sake.

PRECEPTS OF THE CHURCH

1. Assist at Mass on Sundays and Holy Days of obligation.
2. Fast and abstain on the days appointed.

3. Receive the Sacrament of Penance (Reconciliation) at least once a year.
4. Receive Holy Communion at least once a year, during the Easter time.
5. Contribute to the support of the Church.
6. Observe the laws of the Church concerning marriage.

A YOUNG WOMAN'S EXAMINATION OF CONSCIENCE

Responsibilities to God:
Have I gone to Mass on Sunday or have I rebelled and been stubborn about going to Mass?
Did I participate in the Mass or did I daydream?
Have I prayed every day?
Have I read the Bible?
Have I been rebellious toward God and his commands?
Have I misused the name of God by swearing and cursing?
Have I told the Father that I love him for creating me and making me his daughter?
Have I thanked Jesus for becoming man, dying for my sin and rising to give me eternal life?
Have I asked the Holy Spirit to help me conquer sin and temptation and to be obedient to God's commands?

Responsibilities to Others and to Myself:
Have I been rebellious, disobedient or disrespectful to

my parents, teachers and those in authority over me?

Have I lied to or deceived my parents or others?

Have I been arrogant and stubborn?

Have I talked back to my parents or those in authority?

Have I gotten angry, nurtured and held grudges and resentments? Have I refused to forgive others? Have I cultivated hatred?

Have I engaged in sexual fantasies? Have I looked at others lustfully?

Have I read pornographic literature or looked at pornographic pictures, shows or movies?

Have I masturbated?

Have I lustfully kissed or sexually touched someone?

Have I had sexual intercourse?

Have I had an abortion or encouraged another to have one?

Have I gossiped about others? Have I slandered anyone? Have I told lies about others? Have I mocked or made fun of others?

Have I lied or cheated?

Have I stolen anything? Have I paid it back?

Have I been selfish or spiteful towards others?

Have I been jealous?

Have I gotten drunk, or taken drugs?

Have I participated in anything that is of the occult: ouija boards, fortune tellers, seances, channeling, astrology?

Have I been patient, kind, gentle and self-controlled?

When my conscience told me to do something good, did I do it or did I ignore it? *Fr. Thomas Weinandy, OFM., Cap.*
from: Be Reconciled to God

A MARRIED WOMAN'S EXAMINATION OF CONSCIENCE

Responsibilities to God:

Have I gone to Mass every Sunday? Have I participated at Mass or have I daydreamed or been present with a blank mind?
Have I prayed every day (15-20 minutes)?
Have I read the Bible? Have I studied the truths of our faith and allowed them to become more part of the way I think and act? Have I read any spiritual books or religious literature?
Have I told God that I want to love him with my whole heart, mind and strength? Do I hold any resentments toward God?
Have I recognized my need for Jesus and his salvation? Have I asked the Holy Spirit to empower me to live the Christian life, to be a proper wife and parent?
Have I been financially generous to the Church? Have I participated in parish or religious activities?
Have I held resentments toward the Church or Church authorities? Have I forgiven them?

Responsibilities to My Spouse:

Have I cared for my spouse? Have I been generous with my time? Have I been affectionate and loving? Have I told my spouse that I love him?

Have I been concerned about the spiritual well-being of my spouse?

Have I listened to my spouse? Have I paid attention to his concerns, worries and problems? Have I sought these out?

Have I allowed resentments and bitterness toward my spouse to take root in my mind? Have I nurtured these? Have I forgiven my spouse for the wrongs he has committed against me?

Have I allowed misunderstanding, miscommunication, or accidents to cause anger and mistrust? Have I nurtured critical and negative thoughts about my spouse?

Have I manipulated my spouse in order to get my own way? Have I tried to overpower my spouse?

Have I spoken sharply or sarcastically to my spouse? Have I spoken in a demeaning or negative way? Have I injured my spouse through taunting and negative teasing? Have I called my spouse harsh names or used language that is not respectful?

Have I physically abused my spouse?

Have I gossiped about my spouse?

Have I undermined the authority and dignity of my spouse through disrespect and rebelliousness?

Have I been moody and sullen?

Have I bickered with my spouse out of stubbornness and selfishness?

Have I lied or been deceitful to my spouse?

Have I misused sexuality? Have I used sexual relations solely for my own selfish pleasure? Have I been too demanding in my desire for sexual fulfillment? Have I been loving and physically affectionate in my sexual relations or have I used sexual relations in a way that would be demeaning or disrespectful to my spouse? Have I refused sexual relations out of laziness, revenge, or manipulation?

Have I refused to conceive children out of selfishness or material greed? Have I had an abortion or encouraged others to have one?

Have I masturbated?

Have I "flirted" or fostered improper relationships with someone else, either in my mind or through words and actions?

Have I used pornography: books, magazines, or movies?

Have I committed adultery?

Have I misused alcohol or drugs?

Have I been financially responsible?

Responsibilities to Children:

Have I cared for the spiritual needs of my children? Have I been a shepherd and watchman as God has appointed me? Have I tried to foster a Christian family where Jesus is Lord? Have I taught my children the gospel and the commandments of God? Have I prayed with them?

Have I been persistent and courageous in my training and teaching? Have I disciplined them when necessary? Have I been lazy and apathetic?

Have I talked with them to find out their problems, concerns, and fears? Have I been affectionate toward them? Have I hugged them and told them that I love them? Have I played or recreated with them?

Have I been impatient and frustrated with them? Have I corrected them out of love in order to teach them what is right and good? Have I treated them with respect? Have I spoken to them in a sarcastic or demeaning way?

Have I held resentments against them? Have I forgiven them?

Have I been of one heart and mind with my spouse in the upbringing of the children? Or have I allowed disagreements and dissension to disrupt the training, educating and disciplining of our children?

Have I undermined the role of authority in the eyes of my children by speaking negatively against God, the Church, my spouse, or others who hold legitimate authority over them?

Have I been a good Christian witness to my children in what I say and do? Or do I demand one standard for them and another for myself?

Have I been properly generous with my children regarding money and physical and material well-being? Have I been miserly? Have I been extravagant, thus spoiling them?

Responsibilities to Society:
Have I been a Christian witness to those with whom I work or associate? Have I spoken to anyone about the gospel and how important it is to believe in Jesus?
Have I held resentments and anger against those with whom I work, relatives and friends? Have I forgiven them?
Have I been unethical in my business dealings? Have I stolen or lied?
Have I allowed the gospel to influence my political and social opinions?
Have I had a proper Christian concern for the poor and needy?
Have I paid my taxes?
Have I fostered or nurtured hatred toward my "political" enemies either local, national, or international?
Have I been prejudiced toward others because of race, color, religion or social status?

Fr. Thomas Weinandy, OFM. Cap.
from: Be Reconciled to God

Acknowledgments

The compiler and publisher wish to express their gratitude to the following for permission to reproduce or adapt material of which they are the authors, publishers, or copyright holders.

Four prayers, excerpts from *Ad Lib with the Lord* by Mother M. Angelica, © Journey into Scripture 1946. Our Lady of the Angels Monastery, Inc., 5817 Old Leeds Road, Birmingham, Alabama 35210. Reprinted by permission of author.

Eleven prayers from *The Prayer Book of the Saints* by Rev. Charles Dollen, © 1984 by Our Sunday Visitor, Huntington, IN 46750. Reprinted by permission.

Two quotes from *The Heart of Newman* by Fr. E. Przywara, SJ, © 1963. Reprinted by permission. Templegate Publishers, Springfield, Illinois.

Two quotes by Elizabeth Seton from *Elizabeth Seton: Selected Writings*, edited by E. Kelley and A. Melville, © 1987 Paulist Press. Reprinted by permission.

A quote by Hudson Taylor, from *Hudson Taylor's Spiritual Secret* by Mr. and Mrs. Howard Taylor, © 1932, used by permission of Moody Press.

A Young Woman's Examination of Conscience and Married Woman's Examination of Conscience from *Be*

Two prayers from *Eerdman's Book of Famous Prayers, A Treasury of Christian Prayers through the Centuries,* compiled by Veronica Zundel, © 1983 by Lion Publishing, published in America by Wm. B. Eerdman's Publishing and in England by Lion Publishing. Used by permission.

A quote by Corrie ten Boom, from *Each New Day* by Corrie ten Boom, published by World Wide Publications. Used by permission.

Prayers and quotes on Mary from *Virgin Wholly Marvelous,* edited by Peter Brookley, © 1989, published by The Ravengate Press, Still River, MA. Used by permission.

A prayer by Charles T. Webb from *Prayers for a New World* by John W. Suter, published by Charles Scribner's Sons, N.Y., 1984.

A prayer by Ron Klug from *I've Been Thinking,* copyright © 1978, Ausburg Publishing House. Reprinted by permission.

Two prayers by Leslie and Edith Brandt from *Growing Together,* copyright © 1975, Ausburg Publishing House. Reprinted by permission.

A prayer by Judith Mattison from *Prayers from a Mother's Heart,* copyright © 1975, Ausburg Publishing House. Reprinted by permission.

Various prayers from *The New Book of Christian Prayers* edited by Tony Castle, copyright © 1986 by Tony Castle. Reprinted by permission of The Crossroad